SHORTCUT TO ENGLISH COLLOCATIONS

Master 2000+ English Collocations In Used Explained Under 20 Minutes A Day

RACHEL MITCHELL

Copyright © 2017

All rights reserved.

ISBN: 9781520642208

TEXT COPYRIGHT © [RACHEL MITCHELL]

all rights reserved. No part of this guide may be reproduced in any form without permission in writing from the publisher except in the case of brief quotations embodied in critical articles or reviews.

Legal & disclaimer

The information contained in this book and its contents is not designed to replace or take the place of any form of medical or professional advice; and is not meant to replace the need for independent medical, financial, legal or other professional advice or services, as may be required. The content and information in this book have been provided for educational and entertainment purposes only.

The content and information contained in this book have been compiled from sources deemed reliable, and it is accurate to the best of the author's knowledge, information, and belief. However, the author cannot guarantee its accuracy and validity and cannot be held liable for any errors and/or omissions. Further, changes are periodically made to this book as and when needed. Where appropriate and/or necessary, you must consult a professional (including but not limited to your doctor, attorney, financial advisor or such other professional advisor) before using any of the suggested remedies, techniques, or information in this book.

Upon using the contents and information contained in this book, you agree to hold harmless the author from and against any damages, costs, and expenses, including any legal fees potentially resulting from the application of any of the information provided by this book. This disclaimer applies to any loss, damages or injury caused by the use and application, whether directly or indirectly, of any advice or information presented, whether for breach of contract, tort, negligence, personal injury, criminal intent, or under any other cause of action.

You agree to accept all risks of using the information presented inside this book.

You agree that by continuing to read this book, where appropriate and/or necessary, you shall consult a professional (including but not limited to your doctor, attorney, or financial advisor or such other advisor as needed) before using any of the suggested remedies, techniques, or information in this book.

TABLE OF CONTENT

Introduction
What Is a Collocation?
Why Do You Have To Learn Collocations?
Types Of Collocation
Collocations/A
Collocations/B
Collocations/C
Collocations/D
Collocations/E
Collocations/F
Collocations/G
Collocations/H
Collocations/I
Collocations/J
Collocations/K
Collocations/L
Collocations/M
Collocations/N
Collocations/O
Collocations/P
Collocations/Q
Collocations/R
Collocations/S
Collocations/T
Collocations/U
Collocations/V
Collocations/W
Collocations/XYZ
Conclusion
Check Out Other Books

INTRODUCTION

Collocations are the keys to use English more like a native speaker. Learning English Collocations may help students build essential vocabulary and learn to speak more fluent and natural-sounding English.

This book "Shortcut To English Collocations" presents and practices 2000+ collocations in used explained in typical contexts, topics, and in alphabetical order to help students improve their style of written and spoken English. The book is well designed and written by an experienced teacher who has been teaching English for more than 20 years to make sure that all the collocations inside are the most frequent and useful for students at each level.

As the author of this book, I believe that this book will be an indispensable reference and trusted guide for you who may want to use English words in a correct but natural way. Once you read this book, I guarantee you that you will have learned an extraordinarily wide range of useful, and practical English Collocations that will help you become a successful English learner, particularly in examinations such as Cambridge FCE, CAE, CPE, and IELTS; as well as you will even become a successful English user in work and in life within a short period of time only.

Thank you for downloading the book *"Shortcut To English Collocations: Master 2000+ English Collocations In Used Explained Under 20 Minutes A Day."*

Let's get started!

What is a collocation?

A collocation is a pair or group of two or more words that are often used together by native speakers.

Here are some simple examples:

We say: **blond** hair (NOT ~~yellow~~ hair), **make** friends (NOT ~~get~~ friends).

We say: **make** mistakes (NOT ~~do~~ mistakes), **heavy** rain (NOT ~~strong~~ rain).

We say: a **fast** car (NOT a ~~quick~~ car), **do** homework (NOT ~~make~~ homework).

We say: a **quick** meal (NOT a ~~fast~~ meal), **make** an effort (NOT ~~do~~ an effort).

When we make mistakes with collocations, the listeners will usually understand us but our English won't sound natural because it's different from how a native speaker would talk. Therefore, if you want your English to sound natural like native speakers, you have to make efforts to learn collocations since they are difficult to guess.

Why do you have to learn collocations?

Mastering collocations will help you:

- Use the English words more accurately.

- Sound more natural in your English speaking and writing.

- Gain higher scores in academic exams because you know how to express yourself in a variety of ways (vary your speech or your writing).

- Improve your comprehensive reading skills when you read academic books or articles which are written by skillful writers.

Types of Collocation

1. **[Verb + Noun]:** launch a product, play a joke/trick, create opportunities, do homework, make the bed, abuse drugs, accept a challenge, accept an apology, commit murder, etc.

2. **[Verb + Verb]:** can't afford, can't help, can't stand, don't care, don't mind, keep going, make believe, etc.

3. **[Noun + Verb]:** phone rings, lion roars, the plane took off, the bomb went off, etc.

4. **[Noun + Noun]:** action movie, abuse of power, block of flats, contact details, desk job, interest rate, job opportunity, junk food, living conditions, etc.

5. **[Adjective + Noun]:** empty promise, tough question, alternative medicine, bad breath, bad temper, big brother, big money, regular exercise, clean energy, common knowledge, bright future, bright idea, broken home, casual clothes, etc.

6. **[Adjective + Adjective]:** boiling hot, neat and tidy, safe and sound, etc.

7. **[Adverb + Adjective]:** bitterly cold, badly hurt, bitterly disappointed, fully aware, utterly stupid, fast asleep, seriously ill, etc.

8. **[Adverb + Adverb]:** all along, almost certainly, far away, hardly ever, just now, long ago, quite a lot/a bit, right away, straight ahead, quite often, etc.

9. **[Verb + Adverb]:** become increasingly, arrive on time, eat properly, need badly, try hard, do likewise, fight hard, read aloud, whisper softly, vaguely remember, etc.

10. **Phrase:** burst into tears, run out of money, be filled with horror.

COLLOCATIONS/A

A streaming cold *[Adjective + Noun] (a heavy cold.)*

He's got a streaming cold.

She has caught a streaming cold.

She has been in bed with a streaming cold.

A massive heart attack *[Adjective + Noun] (a very serious heart attack.)*

She died of a massive heart attack last year.

No one would like to suffer from a massive heart attack.

Academic year *[Adjective + Noun] (the time during a year when the school is open and students are studying.)*

David is graduating at the end of the academic year with a bachelor degree in law.

The Opening of the Academic Year 2015-2016 took place on Monday.

Attend a school *[Verb + Noun] (to go to a school.)*

It is important for children to attend a school.

Her daughter prefers to attend a school that provides education for females only.

Ancient/ historic monument *[Adjective + Noun] (a very old building, especially one that is an important part of a country's history and is open to visitors)*

The ancient/ historic monument fell down during the bombing.

The ancient monument should be restored immediately.

There are many ancient/ historic monuments in my hometown.

A decline in demand *[Noun + Noun] (a fall in demand.)*

There was a decline in demand for female services in some occupations.

An increase in automobile prices may lead to a decline in demand for gas.

A surge of anger *[Noun + Noun]* *(a powerful rush of an emotion or feeling of anger.)*

Susan felt a surge of anger.

Lucy felt a surge of anger as she watched her ex-husband enter the room with his new girlfriend.

A sense of pride *[Noun + Noun]* *(a feeling of pleasure and satisfaction that you get when you, or someone connected with you, have done or achieved something good.)*

She felt a sense of pride after she had finished the assignment.

Doing well in school gives students a sense of pride.

We have a sense of pride in our community.

Absolutely/utterly ridiculous *[Adverb + Adjective]* *(very silly or completely unreasonable.)*

He looked utterly ridiculous when he dressed like a teenager.

She looks absolutely ridiculous in that yellow hat.

Absolutely/utterly stupid *[Adverb + Adjective]* *(very silly)*

Jack was utterly stupid to quit his job like that.

His behavior was absolutely stupid.

Absolutely/utterly impossible *[Adverb + Adjective]* *(very badly or is extremely difficult to deal with a situation; extremely difficult to achieve something.)*

My cell phone is broken into so many pieces, it'll be absolutely impossible to put it back together again.

It is utterly impossible to dig since the ground is frozen hard.

It's absolutely impossible to climb that mountain.

Absolutely/utterly wrong *[Adverb + Adjective] (completely wrong/ incorrect)*

His answer for that question was absolutely wrong.

That clock is utterly wrong - it's 10.30, not 2.15.

Absolutely/utterly alone *[Adverb + Adjective] (if someone is absolutely/utterly alone, there is no one else with him/her.)*

He was absolutely alone in the house.

She has been utterly alone since her husband died.

Absolutely/utterly convinced *[Adverb + Verb] (completely sure or certain that something is true)*

She is utterly convinced of her husband's innocence.

I'm absolutely convinced that he is lying.

Absolutely/utterly devastated *[Adverb + Verb] (extremely upset and shocked; very sad or unhappy)*

He was absolutely devastated when the doctor told him the news.

Susan was utterly devastated when her husband died.

Absolutely/utterly miserable *[Adverb + Adjective] (extremely unhappy or uncomfortable)*

They were cold, wet, hungry and utterly miserable.

Jane is absolutely miserable living on her own.

Absolutely necessary *[Adverb + Adjective] (totally or completely essential or needed to do something, provide something, or make something happen.)*

The operation is absolutely necessary for him at the moment.

He doesn't want to be disturbed unless something is absolutely necessary.

Abuse drugs *[Verb + Noun] (to use illegal drugs in a way that is harmful to your health)*

Bill has abused drugs for over 5 years.

He died early due to abusing drugs for many years.

Abuse of power *[Noun + Noun] (the harmful, unethical or improper use of authority by someone who has that authority.)*

He was charged with abuse of power to keep prices artificially high.

The president was accused of abusing his power after ordering soldiers to shoot at protesters.

Accept (a) defeat *[Verb + Noun] (to accept the fact that you cannot succeed in doing something and stop trying to do it.)*

He finally had to accept a defeat.

Tom thought he couldn't win the game, so he had to accept a defeat.

Accept a challenge *[Verb + Noun] (to agree to do something difficult or dangerous that needs a lot of skill, energy, and determination to deal with or achieve, especially something you have never done before.)*

It's possible that peter will accept the challenge to be the caption of the football team.

Tom accepted the challenge to climb the high mountain.

Accept an apology *[Verb + Noun] (to forgive someone who says they're sorry for doing something wrong or for causing a problem.)*

They accepted his apologies since his mistake was not serious.

Paul refused to accept his wife's apology and said he wanted a divorce.

Accept an invitation *[Verb + Noun] (to agree to spend time with someone socially or to come to a social event after getting an invitation.)*

Most of the people he invited to his birthday party were happy to accept his invitation.

Tom accepted an invitation to the party.

Accept responsibility *[Verb + Noun]* *(to take the blame for something bad that has happened.)*

He refuses to accept responsibility for the mistake.

Mark accepted responsibility for the failure of the deal.

Alternative energy *[Adjective + Noun]* *(power or electricity produced by using energy from moving water, wind, the sun, and gas from animal waste.)*

It is very important to use alternative energy.

Alternative energy sources include water, wind, the sun, etc.

Alternative medicine *[Adjective + Noun]* *(medical treatments using natural substances and traditional knowledge such as homeopathy and acupuncture, plants instead of artificial drugs and modern surgery.)*

Alternative medicine includes treatments such as homeopathy and acupuncture and hypnotherapy.

A practitioner of alternative medicine gave her some acupuncture and Chinese herbs.

Answer the door *[Verb + Noun]* *(to go and open the door after someone knocks or rings the doorbell.)*

As soon as she heard someone knock, Jessica jumped out of the bed and answered the door.

No-one answered the door although he rang the doorbell many times.

Answer the phone *[Verb + Noun]* *(to pick up a phone that's ringing and talk to the person calling)*

It took him 15 minutes to answer the phone

I called his number, but he didn't answer the phone.

Ask a question *[Verb + Adverb]* *(to ask somebody to tell you something when you want information.)*

The police asked him questions all day.

If you want to ask a question, please raise your hand.

Ask for advice [Verb + Noun] *(to ask someone about what you should do or how you should act in a particular situation.)*

Don't be afraid to ask your teacher for advice on how to prepare for the exam.

Why don't you ask your brother for some advice? He knows all about English.

Note: related collocations include "ask for help" and "ask for suggestions"

Ask for directions [Verb + Noun] *(to ask somebody to show you the way to a particular place.)*

If you don't know which way to go, you can ask for directions.

Her house was not easy to find, I had to ask someone for directions.

Ask permission [Verb + Noun] *(to ask someone in authority, such as your boss, teacher, parent, etc. To give you the right to do something.)*

She always asks her boss's permission for all major expenditure.

Children should ask their parents' permission before playing games.

Above average [Adverb + Adjective] *(more than average; higher or better than the usual amount or level esp. In amount, age, height, weight, etc.)*

The teacher said that her children are of above average intelligence.

She is above average height.

Advertising campaign [Noun + Noun] *(a series of advertisements that will be used to promote a product or service.)*

The advertising campaign has generated a lot of sales for our company.

We've just launched our new nationwide advertising campaign.

Achieve a goal *[Verb + Noun] (to do something that you'd planned or hoped to achieve.)*

I think she will be able to achieve her goal of losing ten kilos before Christmas.

He hasn't yet reached his goal of buying the house of 1 million dollars.

Active ingredient *[Adjective + Noun] (the chemically active part of a drug, medicine or pesticide that makes it work.)*

What's the active ingredient in this chemical compound?

Do you know what the active ingredient in aspirin is?

Admit defeat *[Verb + Noun] (to accept that you can't achieve a goal or succeed in doing something and stop trying to do it.)*

He never admits defeat before a game's over, no matter how far behind he is.

Mark couldn't fix the car himself, so he admitted defeat and called a mechanic.

Against the law *[Adjective + Noun] (illegal; not allowed by the law/rules)*

Selling drugs is against the law.

It will be against the law if you park your car here overnight.

All along *[Adverb + Adverb] (all the time; from the very beginning)*

I think she's been cheating us all along.

He realized it was in his pocket all along.

He knew all along that it wasn't her real name.

Almost certainly *[Adverb + Adverb] (almost definitely)*

I think Susan will almost certainly get the job.

Without operation, he will almost certainly die.

Alphabetical order *[Adjective + Noun] (an order based on the letters of an alphabet, with "a" being the first and "z" being the last in English.)*

He neatly arranged his books in alphabetical order.

The children put the words in alphabetical order.

Not…anymore/ any longer adverb + adverb to say that a situation has ended or someone has stopped doing something

I couldn't wait any longer.

She doesn't want to see him anymore.

They don't live there anymore. They've already moved to New York.

Apply for a job *[Verb + Noun] (to make an official request for a job)*

He has applied for many jobs this week.

It's really hard to get this job because so many people apply for it.

Arrive on time *[Verb + Adverb] (to arrive at the correct time and not late.)*

The plane arrived was on time.

Don't worry, David will arrive on time.

Attract attention *[Verb + Noun] (to make someone notice you or something)*

Movies with excellent actors and actresses always attract great attention.

He has tried to attract her attention, but she hasn't noticed him yet.

An awful lot *[Adjective + Noun] (a very large amount)*

His wife has spent an awful lot of money on clothes these days.

John is a famous lawyer. He gets an awful lot of clients.

Ancient history *[Adjective + Noun] (things that happened a long time ago and no longer new, interesting, important or relevant.)*

We are studying ancient history.

My father and my grandfather are very interested in ancient history.

The origins of these customs are still unknown. They lost somewhere in ancient history.

Antique jewelry *[Adjective + Noun] (jewelry that is old and valuable.)*

My mom is interested in collecting antique jewelry.

My uncle became rich from selling antique jewelry.

Aisle seat *[Noun + Noun] (a seat in a train, plane which is next to an aisle.)*

Would you like an aisle seat or a window seat?

I'd like an aisle seat in the smoking section, please.

Attend classes *[Verb + Noun] (to go regularly to classes.)*

Many students attend classes all day and work all night.

If you attend classes regularly, you will be making good progress.

Aches and pains *[Noun + Noun] (minor pains that are continuous and unpleasant due to physical work or old age, but usually not very serious.)*

His grandma complains about all her aches and pains in her back and shoulders usually.

Tom is tired of hearing about all her grandma's aches and pains.

You might have all sorts of aches and pains when you get older.

Action movie *[Noun + Noun] (a film/movie that contains lots of action and violence)*

Jack has loved action movies since he was a teenager.

Action movies and horror films are my favourite genres.

Apartment block *[Noun + Noun] (a large building that's divided into many* *apartments/flats.)*

They live in an apartment block just down the street.

There was a fire in that apartment block but luckily no one got hurt.

A slave to fashion [Noun + Noun] *(someone who is influenced too much by fashion.)*

Unlike most young people, I'm not a slave to fashion.

Are you a slave to fashion?

Adoring fans [Adjective + Noun] *(fans who show much love to a particular band or singer.)*

The band used to be worshiped by adoring fans all over the world.

The movie star is mobbed by adoring fans wherever he goes.

Air quality [Noun + Noun] *(a measurement of the cleanliness of the air in a particular place.)*

The air quality in our area has become worse in the last few months.

The local authority must take measures to improve the city's air quality.

Advertising agency [Noun + Noun] *(a company that creates, plans, and handles advertisements for its clients.)*

Peter works for an advertising agency in London.

His advertising agency was established in 2005 in New York.

Advertising budget [Noun + Noun] *(the amount of money a company is willing to pay for advertising.)*

Our company's advertising budget has increased dramatically recently.

His company spent most of the advertising budget on YouTube and Facebook.

Arms dealer [Noun + Noun] *(a person or an organization that sells military* weapons.)

He wishes to become a leading international arms dealer.

The suspected arms dealers were arrested in Florida.

Acute illness *[Adjective + Noun]* *(any illness that develops quickly. It may be severe and last a relatively short period of time.)*

She died of an acute illness.

Her father dropped dead of an acute illness.

Air/sea/rail/bus/coach/car travel *[Noun + Noun]* *(the activity of travelling by air/sea/rail/bus/coach/car.)*

Air travel is fast, but sea travel is restful.

Car travel is worse than train travel.

Act within the law *[Verb + Noun]* *(not do illegal things)*

The police officers must act within the law.

Doctors and lawyers must act within the law.

Appear in court *[Verb + Noun]* *(to go to a court of law.)*

Mr. Johnson will appear in court on Tuesday next week.

She was summoned to appear in court to give testimony.

Ask a favor *[Verb + Noun]* *(to ask somebody to do something for you because you need their help, support or approval of something.)*

Can/could/may I ask you a favor?

I would like to ask a favor of you.

A tough choice *[Adjective + Noun]* *(a difficult choice.)*

It was a tough choice for him between two firms he really enjoyed.

This was a tough choice for her to make on her own, even if she was already twenty-five.

It was a tough choice for her to choose between the two universities, and at last, she chose Harvard.

COLLOCATIONS/B

Bright child *[Adjective + Noun] (an intelligent or clever child.)*

A bright child is usually curious about life.

Her son seems to be a bright child.

Be off the beaten track *[Phrase] (be in a place where few people visit.)*

The great vacation spot we found was completely off the beaten track.

We stayed in a nice little Italian restaurant which was completely off the beaten track.

Broach a subject *[Verb + Noun] (to start talking about a sensitive subject.)*

Tom decided to broach the subject of a pay rise with his employer.

Sarah was afraid to broach the subject of starting a divorce to her abusive husband.

Bring up the subject *[Verb + Noun] (to deliberately start talking about a subject.)*

She found it difficult to bring up the subject of money with her children.

She decided to bring up the subject of her cancer with her husband.

Break an agreement *[Verb + Noun] (to not do what someone has to do according to an agreement.)*

Alice was worried that she might be breaking the agreement.

Tom broke the agreement made between him and Peter.

Boost sales/ profits *[Verb + Noun] (to improve or increase sales/ profits.)*

We are making an attempt to boost our sales/ profits.

They have boosted their sales/profits beyond their expectations.

Bear in mind *[Phrase] (to remember.)*

Bear in mind that I can't run as fast as you.

We should bear in mind that time is money.

Bear in mind that he is not as young as he was, so don't walk so fast.

Basic human needs *[Adjective + Noun] (the elements required for survival, such as food, water, shelter, etc.)*

Money helps us meet our basic human needs.

Employees can meet their human basic needs if their salary is good.

Broaden/ expand/ widen sb's horizons *[Verb + Noun] (to increase the range of interests, activities, and knowledge.)*

Travelling definitely broadens your horizons.

He likes to use technology to expand his horizons.

Be overburdened with something *[Phrase] (to give somebody/something too much work to deal with)*

He is often overburdened with work.

She has been overburdened with troubles recently.

Bitterly cold *[Adverb + Adjective] (extremely and unpleasant cold.)*

Winters in London tend to be bitterly cold.

It was bitterly cold outside last night.

Bitterly disappointed *[Adverb + Adjective] (extremely disappointed.)*

She was bitterly disappointed at the result of the test.

If Tom doesn't pass the final exam, he'll be bitterly disappointed.

Be in pain *[Phrase] (if someone is in pain, he/she feels pain in a part of their body, because they are injured or ill.)*

Are you in pain somewhere?

I don't know what to say to her when she's in pain.

Blissfully unaware *[Adverb + Adjective] (a state in which you do not know or realize that something unpleasant or worrying is happening or that something exists.)*

They were blissfully unaware of the danger.

Tom's parents remained blissfully unaware of his plans to leave home.

Badly need *[Adverb + Verb] (need something very much.)*

They badly need the money.

He badly needs a vacation.

She badly needs to clean her room.

Bitterly disappointing *[Adverb + Adjective] (making someone feel extremely disappointed.)*

What a bitterly disappointing result!

This year's sales figures were bitterly disappointing.

Bitterly resent *[Adverb + Verb] (to feel extremely angry about something, especially because you have been forced to accept it.)*

She bitterly resents being treated like a maid.

Susan bitterly resented the new woman in her father's life.

Bitterly criticize *[Adverb + Verb] (to express that you strongly disapprove of somebody/something; to express your extreme disapproval of someone or something.)*

His decision was bitterly criticized by his parents.

The government has been bitterly criticized for not tackling the problem seriously.

Bitterly regret *[Adverb + Verb] (to feel very sorry about something sad or wrong you have done or a mistake that you have made.)*

The airline bitterly regretted any inconvenience caused by the delay.

She bitterly regrets what she said.

Bitterly complain *[Adverb + Verb] (to say that you are very annoyed, unhappy or not satisfied about someone or something.)*

Mark bitterly complained that his boss was unfair and useless.

Many people bitterly complained about the noise.

Bitterly cry *[Adverb + Verb] (to produce a lot of tears from someone's eyes as the result of a strong negative emotion, such as unhappiness or pain.)*

Julie bitterly cried when she got the letter.

Tom bitterly cried as he saw these images.

Be exposed to infection *[Phrase] (to be infected with a virus.)*

He was exposed to infection when he studied in Sydney.

She was exposed to infection while vacationing in London.

Become/get pregnant *[Verb + Adjective] (if a woman becomes pregnant, she is having a baby developing inside her body.)*

Jane stopped smoking when she became pregnant.

Mary has been trying to get pregnant for 2 years now.

Become involved *[Verb + Adjective] (to take part in something (an activity, event, or situation); being part of something or connected with something.)*

He would like to become involved in politics

We would like to become involved in raising funds for building the church.

Become depressed *[Verb + Adjective] (feel very unhappy, very sad and without hope because of a difficult or unpleasant situation.)*

She became depressed after her husband's death.

He became deeply depressed when he got fired from his first job.

Become famous [Verb + Adjective] (to be known and recognized by many people)

She became famous for her novels

He became famous as a lawyer.

Become angry = get angry [Verb + Adjective] (to feel very annoyed)

She became really angry with the kids.

He was very angry with himself for making a stupid mistake.

Below average [Adverb + Adjective] (worse than average)

Bill considers himself to be below average.

Teachers and parents should pay more attention to below average children.

Back pay [Adjective + Noun] (money that is owed to an employee in the past but that has not been paid yet.)

The company still owe those workers a total of approximately $800,000 in back pay.

How much back pay does the company still owe their employees?

Back road [Adjective + Noun] (a small road that is away from any main roads and does not have much traffic on it.)

There was too much traffic on the highway, so we used a back road instead.

Those back roads don't have signs, so they will probably get lost if they don't have a map.

Back street [Adjective + Noun] (a street that's away from any main streets or business areas of a town or a city.)

Her shop is on a little back street behind the post office.

Jane lives on a little back street on the other side of town.

Back taxes *[Adjective + Noun] (taxes that haven't been paid when they were due.)*

Bill owes more than $400,000 in back taxes.

You have to pay a fine if pay all your back taxes late.

Bad breath *[Adjective + Noun] (breath that smells unpleasant)*

The worst thing about my new boyfriend is his bad breath.

If you don't want your breath to be so bad, you should clean your teeth more often.

Bad habit *[Adjective + Noun] (unhealthy habit; a habit that badly affects you or other people.)*

My uncle has a bad habit of smoking too much.

Jessica has a bad habit of staying up too late.

Bad loser *[Adjective + Noun] (someone who behaves badly when they lose.)*

Tom is a bad loser. Nobody likes him.

He's a bad loser. He always behaves badly when he is defeated.

Bad mood *[Adjective + Noun] (an angry or irritable state of mind.)*

Mark has been in a bad mood all day.

Dad is in a bad mood today, so be careful what you are going to say to him.

Bad temper *[Adjective + Noun] (a tendency to become angry quickly and easily)*

Bill's got a really bad temper. Jane would not marry bill if she knows he has a really bad temper.

Jane's husband has a bad temper. He sometimes beats her and children when he gets really mad.

Badly damaged *[Adverb + Verb] (to do a lot of damage to something which makes it less attractive, useful or valuable.)*

Their houses were badly damaged in the storm.

The roof was badly damaged by strong winds.

Her flat was badly damaged by a fire.

Badly hurt *[Adverb + Verb] (seriously injured or in pain)*

My grandmother's back has been badly hurting her recently.

Strong light badly hurts her eyes.

Break up *[Phrase] (to end a marriage or a romantic relationship with someone.)*

Bill and his girlfriend broke up after an argument.

Jane's just broken up with her boyfriend.

Peter broke up with carol and started dating Susan.

Balance a budget *[Verb + Noun] (to spend no more money than you receive; to make income and expenditure equal in a budget.)*

Bob try to balance his budget, but he still gets into debt.

The government is supposed to balance the budget by raising taxes.

Balanced diet *[Adjective + Noun] (a diet that contains adequate amounts of the nutrients necessary for good health.)*

Eating a balanced diet is one of the most important things everyone should try.

If you need to live healthily, you should eat a balanced diet.

Bare essentials *[Adjective + Noun] (the most basic and necessary things)*

There wasn't much time, so he just packed the bare essentials.

A majority of people lack the bare essentials in India.

Barely able to do something *[Phrase] (used for saying that it is possible for someone to do something but only with difficulty.)*

She was barely able to see the bridge in the fog.

His mother was barely able to read and write.

After drinking too much, he was barely able to walk.

Basic right *[Adjective + Noun] (a fundamental right that a person or an animal has.)*

Liberty, equality, and freedom of thought and expression are basic rights in most societies.

It is widely argued that animals also have some basic rights.

Bear a resemblance (to sb/sth) *[Verb + Noun] (to be similar to, look like somebody or something.)*

Bill bears a striking resemblance to his father.

This watch bears a strong resemblance to the one he lost last week.

Break a record = beat a record *[Verb + Noun] (to do something that is better, faster, longer, etc. than it has been previously done or achieved; to achieve a better result than there has ever been before.)*

Jessica won the gold medal, and she broke the record for the 5,500 meters.

The painting has broken the record, selling for over £30 million.

Become increasingly *[Verb + Adverb] (to become more and more over a period of time.)*

The internet is becoming increasingly important in people's daily lives.

This situation has become increasingly difficult.

Best friends *[Adjective + Noun] (closest friends)*

Paul and mark were best friends in college.

We were best friends in high school.

Cathy is my best friend - we've known each other since we were teenagers.

Broaden/expand/widen somebody's horizons *[Verb + Noun]* *(to increase or expand the range of interests, activities, and knowledge that somebody has experienced or knows about.)*

Travelling has really helped to broaden his horizons.

The trip to Europe has certainly broadened my horizons.

Big brother *[Adjective + Noun]* *(older brother)*

My big brother is a doctor.

Jane's big brother is very kind. He is always willing to help any person who needs his help.

Big sister *[Adjective + Noun]* *(older sister)*

Lucy's big sister is smaller than her, but three years older.

Sometimes my big sister helps me to do chores.

Big decision *[Adjective + Noun]* *(very important decision)*

Studying overseas was the first big decision he made.

Think carefully before you make any big decision.

Big money *[Adjective + Noun]* *(a large amount of money)*

My father makes big money in real estate.

If you're not prepared to take risks, you'll never make big money.

Bitterly cold *[Adverb + Adjective]* *(extremely and unpleasantly cold.)*

Winters in London are bitterly cold.

It was a bitterly cold night.

Blind faith *[Adjective + Noun]* *(unquestioning belief in something, even when it's unreasonable or wrong.)*

Don't live with blind faith.

Students seemed to accept everything he said with blind faith.

Blind obedience [Adjective + Noun] *(unquestioning obedience, even when you're told to do something you know is wrong or unreasonable.)*

Workers did wrong things by following orders with blind obedience.

Blind obedience may lead to unforeseen and perhaps unfortunate results.

Blissful ignorance [Adjective + Noun] *(a state in which someone is unaware of something unpleasant or worrying, so it does not make him/her unhappy.)*

Paul's parents remained in blissful ignorance of his plans to drop out of high school.

All the time his business was failing, peter's wife and family remained in blissful ignorance of his lung cancer.

Blanket of snow [Noun + Noun] *(a thick covering layer of snow.)*

A blanket of snow covered the ground.

The street was covered by a blanket of snow covered.

Business trip [Noun + Noun] *(a trip made somewhere and back again for business reasons.)*

Bill is away on a business trip.

I will make a business trip to japan next month.

Boat trip [Noun + Noun] *(a journey or excursion to a place in a boat, usually for pleasure.)*

Today is a great day for a boat trip around the lake.

We took a boat trip to the islands last weekend.

Block of flats [Noun + Noun] *(a large building that is divided into flats or apartments on several levels or floors.)*

A new block of flats is going to be built in this area next month.

His house is on the 3rd floor of that block of flats.

Blow your nose *[Verb + Noun]* *(to clean your nose by forcing air through it into a cloth or a piece of soft paper.)*

She took out some tissues and blew her nose.

She had a terrible cold and spent much time blowing her nose.

Break a promise *[Verb + Noun]* *(to fail to do what you said that you would do.)*

Tom broke his promise and kept going to the casino.

Jane broke her promise to return the book to me.

Break the news *[Verb + Noun]* *(to tell somebody some important news, usually bad news.)*

The doctor gently broke the news to Cathy about her husband's cancer.

David tried to break the news of Jane mother's death to her gently.

Breaking news *[Verb + Noun]* *(current news that a media organization gives special or live coverage to)*

I was watching the game when some breaking news came on, so I missed Mario's goal.

We interrupt this broadcast with some breaking news about the crisis in the Middle East.

Bright future *[Adjective + Noun]* *(successful or happy future)*

Mark has a bright future in athletics.

This young author has a bright future.

Bright idea *[Adjective + Noun]* *(a clever idea, thought or plan.)*

I hope that peter will have some bright ideas for us.

My company needs employees full of bright ideas.

Breathtaking scenery *[Adjective + Noun]* *(extremely impressive, striking and beautiful views.)*

We floated down a river in a canoe and enjoyed the breathtaking scenery.

People enjoy visiting Barujari mountain because of its breathtaking scenery.

Bring about changes *[Verb + Noun]* *(to cause or create changes in a situation.)*

John is working to bring about changes in the food industry.

What brought about changes in bill's attitude?

Bring something to someone's attention *[Verb + Noun]* *(to make people notice or aware of something, often something that causes problems.)*

I would be grateful if you bring it to my attention.

We should bring this problem to his attention.

Bring something to an end = bring something to a close *[Verb + Noun]* *(to make something finish; to end or stop something.)*

I think it is time to bring the meeting to an end.

The conflict has been brought to a close.

Bring someone to justice *[Verb + Noun]* *(to put someone on trial in court in order to find out whether he/she is guilty of a crime.)*

The man's killers have been brought to justice.

The police officer arrested and brought the thief to justice.

Budget deficit *[Noun + Noun]* *(the amount by which actual expenses are greater than planned expenses in a particular period of time.)*

He is facing a budget deficit and may not be able to take on any new projects for a long time.

The president has been working hard to try to balance out the budget deficit.

Background music *[Noun + Noun]* (music that is played while something else is going on so that people do not actively attend to it.)

I loved the background music in the video. It was great!

Background music is very beneficial in classrooms.

Below freezing *[Adverb + Adjective]* (below 0° Celsius.)

The temperature has remained below freezing point for several days.

The temperature dropped below freezing this morning.

Boiling hot *[Adjective + Adjective]* (extremely hot.)

This soup is boiling hot.

It's been boiling hot recently.

Brand name *[Noun + Noun]* (a name that is given and used by a company to its product or service.)

These products are sold under different brand names throughout the world.

When it comes to soft drinks, Coca-Cola is the most valuable brand name in the world.

Be (good) value for money *[Phrase]* (to be well worth the money.)

This car is really good value for money.

The five-star hotel was good value for money.

Be out of condition *[Phrase]* (not be healthy or fit due to lack of exercise.)

Many women are out of condition due to the lack of exercise.

If you don't want to be out of condition, you must exercise regularly.

Be hard of hearing *[Phrase]* (not able to hear well.)

The old man is a bit hard of hearing.

My grandmother is quite old now and she's increasingly hard of hearing.

Become extinct [Verb + Adjective] (to be no longer in existence.)

The numbers of these animals have become extinct these days.

As far as people concern, the giant panda will soon become extinct.

Be under threat [Phrase] (to be in danger or at risk of becoming extinct.)

Wildlife has been under threat from a variety of human activities.

We're fighting to protect animals that are under threat.

Be the life and soul of the party [Phrase] (someone who is very lively and entertaining at social events.)

Tom became the life of the party after he had gotten a few beers.

Jack is an extroverted man. He is always the life and soul of the party.

Balance the books [Verb + Noun] (if you balance your books, you show that the amount of money you have spent is equal to the amount that you have received.)

After buying a new house, David had to work some extra hours in order to balance the books.

The accountant spent a couple of days trying to balance the books of the company.

Bend over backwards [Verb + Adverb] (to try very hard or make a special effort to do something in order to help or please someone.)

I bent over backwards to help her.

Alice bent over backwards to accommodate her customers.

Bachelor's degree [Noun + Noun] (the first degree that you get when you finish a 3-4 year course at a college or university.)

John earned a bachelor's degree in technology and a master's degree of science.

It took him six years to get his bachelor's degree in French.

Boarding school *[Noun + Noun] (a school at which pupils are provided with living accommodation during the school term.)*

David is about going to a boarding school in England.

Cheryl sent her daughter to a boarding school in the north.

Brand awareness *[Noun + Noun] (the extent to which consumers are aware of the particular brand of a product or service.)*

You need to build good brand awareness so that people could know well your products and business.

We can use social media to increase brand awareness of our products.

Brand loyalty *[Noun + Noun] (the tendency of some customers to keep buying the same brand of goods rather than to try other brands.)*

Brand loyalty plays a vital role in many customers' buying habits.

Most manufacturers would like to improve brand loyalty to their products.

Book genre *[Noun + Noun] (a particular type of book that you can recognize based on its special features.)*

What is your favorite book genre?

Her favorite book genre is mystery, but her boyfriend loves science fiction.

Best-selling book *[Noun + Noun] (a book that is extremely popular and has been sold in a very large quantity.)*

The famous author wants to create another best-selling book.

His best-selling book has been published for almost 6 months.

Be called for an interview *[Verb + Noun] (if you are called for an interview, you're invited to attend an interview.)*

She was called for an interview last week.

I hope that I will be called for an interview when I send them my resume.

Be one's own boss *[Phrase]* *(if you are your own boss, you are self-employed.)*

Since my father is his own boss, his time is flexible.

Do you like to be your own boss?

Be stuck behind a desk *[Phrase]* *(to be unhappy with a job which is all desk work.)*

I couldn't stand the thought of being stuck behind a desk all day.

He dislikes being stuck behind a desk - he'd prefer to work outside

Be/get stuck in a rut *[Phrase]* *(to be in a boring, repetitive job that is difficult to change.)*

You should change your job if you're stuck in a rut.

Tom gave up his job because he felt he got stuck in a rut.

Be well-paid *[Verb + Adjective]* *(if your job is well-paid, you earn a lot of money for the work that you do.)*

His job is very well paid, and he enjoys it a lot.

Jack did the work well, and he was well paid.

A nurse is not as well paid as a doctor.

Be slightly different *[Verb + Adjective]* *(be a bit different.)*

You may be right, but your opinion is slightly different to mine.

British English is slightly different to American English.

Be engrossed in *[Phrase]* *(if you are engrossed in something, you feel so interested and give it all your attention.)*

Jane was so engrossed in the movie that she didn't hear the phone ring.

Tom was so engrossed in his book that he forgot his dinner.

Bedtime reading [Noun + Noun] *(something such as a book or magazine that you read at bedtime.)*

The bible is my mother's favourite bedtime reading.

Mark twain stories have become his favourite bedtime reading.

What is your favourite bedtime reading?

Box office hit [Adjective + Noun] *(a popular and financially successful film, play, or actor.)*

The film "titanic" was a huge box office hit in 1997.

The movie "stomp in the yard" became a box office hit of the year.

Be heavy-going [Verb + Adjective] *(if a book, a play, or a film is heavy going, it is boring and difficult to read or understand.)*

The novel is a bit heavy going at the beginning.

I found the book really heavy going.

Be a bit off-colour [Verb + Adjective] *(if you are a bit off-colour, you feel slightly ill (not as well as usual))*

Bill has been a bit off-colour recently.

He decided not to go to the concert because he felt a bit off colour.

Be at death's door [Phrase] *(if someone is at death's door, he/she is very ill and likely to die.)*

He was at death's door when his blood cancer was finally diagnosed.

She was sick, but she was not at death's door.

Be on the mend [Phrase] *(to be recovering or getting better after an illness or injury.)*

His broken leg is gradually on the mend.

She's had a cold, but she's on the mend now.

Be under the weather *[Phrase] (if you are under the weather, you do not feel well.)*

I'm a bit under the weather now, so please don't ask me to cook dinner.

I've been feeling a little under the weather recently - I think I'm getting ill.

Be as fit as a fiddle *[Phrase] (if you are as fit as a fiddle, you are very healthy and full of energy.)*

Peter seems to be as fit as a fiddle.

My grandfather is 85, but he is as fit as a fiddle.

Back up files *[Verb + Noun] (to prepare a second copy of a file so that it can be used if the original is lost or damaged.)*

Remember to back up your files every two days.

We recommend that you should back up your files onto a floppy disk since all files saved in your computer might be lost or deleted unexpectedly.

Boot up *[Phrase] (to begin operating or start up a computer.)*

I'm waiting for my computer to boot up.

My computer crashed and now it doesn't boot up anymore.

Bookmark a web page *[Verb + Noun] (to mark or record the address of a web page so that you can find it easily for future reference.)*

Can you show me how to bookmark a web page on iPhone?

I always bookmark a web page when I find one I like.

Browse websites *[Verb + Noun] (to look at or to look for information on specific websites.)*

If you want to browse websites, you must have your computer connected to the internet.

John usually browses websites to get useful information that he can use for his writing.

Bonus payment *[Noun + Noun] (an extra amount of money that is given to an employee in addition to their wage or salary as a reward for excellent work.)*

I was entitled to the bonus payment.

The employees' bonus payment depends on how excellent their work performance is.

Basic salary *[Adjective + Noun] (the amount of money that someone earns for a particular work period, not including any extra payments such as bonuses and overtime.)*

He earns a basic salary of $20,000 per year.

As a sales person, you'll earn a basic salary of $550 per month plus commission of 5% on sales you make.

Back garden *[Adjective + Noun] (a garden which is located at the rear of the house.)*

The children were playing in the garden.

He was in the back garden cutting the grass.

Be in the black *[Phrase] (if a person or an organization is in the black, they have money in the bank and are not in debt (as opposed to "in the red"))*

His company has managed to stay in the black for over 2 years.

Sally wishes her accounts were in the black.

Be in the red *[Phrase] (if a person or an organization is in the red, they owe money to the bank.)*

His company is in the red all the time.

My bank account is in the red.

Be in a relationship *[Phrase] (to have a sexual or romantic relationship with someone.)*

I'm not sure if Rosie is in a relationship right now.

Sarah told her boyfriend that she didn't want to be in a relationship with him any longer.

Be (just) good friends *[Phrase]* *(used to say that someone is not having a romantic relationship with someone else.)*

"Are you in a relationship with carol?" "No, we're just good friends."

Tom's mother doesn't seem to believe that Mary and he are just good friends.

Be on commission *[Phrase]* *(to pay someone an extra amount of money from sales they have made or for work they have done.)*

The hours we work don't matter because we are on commission.

Any salesperson who is on commission earns 10% of the total amount he/she sells.

Be on-trend *[Phrase]* *(to be very fashionable/ to be in keeping with the latest fashions.)*

Her fashion designs are really on-trend.

His haircut style is so on-trend.

Be over-populated *[Verb + Adjective]* *(if a country or city is overpopulated, it has too many people living in it.)*

China is over-populated.

Big cities tend to be quite over-populated.

Be getting on a bit *[Phrase]* *(if you are getting on a bit, you are getting old.)*

She's getting on a bit - she'll be 75 next birthday.

My parents are getting on a bit now. They don't get around as well as they used to.

Be dressed to kill *[Phrase]* *(if someone is dressed to kill, they are intentionally wearing very fancy or attractive clothes to make people notice them.)*

Rosie was really dressed to kill at the party last night.

Lucy was dressed to kill for her date on Friday night.

Breathtaking view *[Adjective + Noun] (a view which is extremely beautiful or impressive.)*

We have never seen such a breathtaking view of the mountains.

Our hotel room had a breathtaking view of New York harbor.

Broad shoulders *[Adjective + Noun] (wide shoulders.)*

He is a tall man with broad shoulders.

Tom has broad shoulders because he exercises and lifts weights.

Bright smile *[Adjective + Noun] (a cheerful and lively smile.)*

Carol gave me a bright smile.

Alice favored him with a very bright smile.

Bushy eyebrows *[Adjective + Noun] (thick and shaggy eyebrows.)*

Her boyfriend has bushy eyebrows.

He lowered his bushy eyebrows at tom.

Jack has a gentle face with bushy eyebrows.

Button nose *[Adjective + Noun] (a small round nose.)*

He touched her button nose.

That was a boy with short curly hair and a button nose.

Beer belly *[Adjective + Noun] (a fat stomach because of drinking a lot of beer over a long period.)*

He was a short and fat man with a large beer belly.

He is tired of people laughing at his beer belly.

Be stuck in traffic *[Phrase] (if you are stuck in traffic, you are in a traffic jam and therefore your vehicle is not moving or moving very slowly.)*

We got stuck in a traffic jam this morning.

He got to the airport late since his taxi was stuck in traffic.

Be full up [Verb + Adjective] *(to eat or drink so much that you can no longer eat or drink anymore.)*

"Would you like some more food?" "No, thanks. I'm full up".

He was full up after eating too many cookies.

Bolt something down [Phrase] *(to eat or swallow food very quickly.)*

Tom was so hungry that he bolted his food down

Jane bolted down her breakfast and rushed out to work.

Be dying of hunger [Phrase] *(to be very hungry (an exaggerated way of saying someone is hungry).*

I'm dying of hunger. Do you have anything to eat?

Thousands of children are dying of hunger every day in this world.

Broken home [Phrase] *(a family in which the parents are divorced or do not live together.)*

That girl comes from a broken home.

Bill came from a broken home, but he studied hard and became a lawyer.

Bring up a family = raise a family [Verb + Noun] *(to take care of or bring up children in a family setting.)*

Julie got married and raised a family before she became a doctor.

Bringing up a family is supposed to be a challenge for most married couple.

Be/fall desperately in love [Phrase] *(to be incredibly in love with a person, but that person does not share the same feelings.)*

Jack was desperately in love with Lucy.

A young woman falls desperately in love with the man she has desired all her life.

Blissfully happy *[Adverb + Adjective]* (*extremely or completely happy.*)

Tom was blissfully happy to see Mary again.

Alice was blissfully happy when she visited her grandmother in London.

Bitterly disappointed = extremely disappointed *[Adverb + Adjective]* (*extremely unhappy or upset because somebody or something was not as good as you hoped or expected.*)

He was bitterly disappointed by the quality of the wine.

They were bitterly disappointed at the result of the world cup final.

If my brother doesn't get the job, he'll be bitterly disappointed.

Brilliant career *[Verb + Noun]* (*an extremely successful career.*)

He seemed to have a brilliant career at Harvard.

Lionel Messi has a brilliant career as a football player.

Bumpy flight *[Adjective + Noun]* (*an uncomfortable and rough flight, usually because of bad weather.*)

After a long and bumpy flight, we arrived at the Boston Logan international airport.

Was it a smooth or a bumpy flight?

Break the law *[Verb + Noun]* (*to fail to obey a law; to act contrary to a law; to do something illegal.*)

You will break the law if you drive the wrong way on a one-way street.

He was arrested because he broke the law.

Bitter dispute *[Adjective + Noun]* (*a dispute with a lot of anger and hatred.*)

We had a bitter dispute over money.

She had a bitter dispute with her mother over her mother's decision to sell the house.

Be in agreement [Phrase] (to have the same opinion.)

I'm glad they both are in agreement.

We are all in agreement that Mr. Johnson should resign.

Be deeply offensive [Adverb + Adjective] (to make someone extremely resentful, upset, or annoyed.)

Such pictures were deeply offensive to some people.

The article was deeply offensive to many politicians.

The advertisement was offensive to many women.

Be the love of someone's life [Phrase] (to be loved by a person more than any other person at any time in life.)

Peter was the love of her life.

Mary has always been the love of his life.

Be mature enough to live independently [Phrase] (be old enough to live independently.)

Her son is mature enough to live independently on his own income.

If our children finish university, they will be mature enough to live independently on their own salary.

Board the plane [Verb + Noun] (to get onto an aircraft.)

They asked passengers to board the plane by walking through this indoor bridge.

Passengers with small children will be allowed to board the plane first.

COLLOCATIONS/C

Cost someone a great deal of money *[Phrase]* *(cost someone a lot of money)*

The advertising campaign costs us a great deal of money.

Pursuing higher education in Harvard University costs students a great deal of money.

Crowded streets *[Adjective + Noun]* *(streets that are full of people.)*

He doesn't like having to navigate New York's crowded streets.

We walked quickly through the crowded streets.

Circle of friends *[Adjective + Noun]* *(a number of close friends who meet regularly to do things together as a group.)*

We have a large circle of friends and acquaintances.

He is one of my close circle of friends.

Critically ill *[Adverb + Adjective]* *(extremely/dangerously ill.)*

He became critically ill and were awaiting surgery.

He begged her to take care of him because he was critically ill.

Constructive criticism *[Adjective + Noun]* *(useful or helpful criticism.)*

He always welcomes constructive criticism of his work.

She asked her teacher for some constructive criticism of her essay before she tried to revise it.

Come up with an idea *[Verb + Noun]* *(to think of an idea.)*

He is broke. He has to come up with an idea for making money.

Mary's always coming up with interesting ideas.

He came up with an idea for starting his business.

Carry on a conversation = Hold a conversation *[Verb + Noun] (to talk between two or more people to exchange news, feelings, and thoughts.)*

We could hardly hold/carry on a conversation with all the noise in the background.

It's impossible to hold/carry on a conversation with so many distractions.

Call a meeting *[Verb + Noun] (to order or invite people to assemble for a meeting; to request people to hold a meeting.)*

Our CEO has called a meeting to discuss the new business project.

They called a meeting to discuss important political issues.

Chair a committee/ meeting *[Verb + Noun] (to be in charge of a committee/ meeting.)*

He was appointed to chair the committee/ meeting.

He was invited to chair the committee/ meeting.

Call someone names *[Verb + Noun] (to call somebody by an abusive or offensive name; to use rude or insulting words to describe someone.)*

Tom became angry when the other classmates called him names.

Peter was punished for calling his teacher names.

Call someone's name *[Verb + Noun] (to say someone's name loudly)*

When I call your name, say "yes".

Jack was wondering why his name wasn't called.

Call a strike *[Verb + Noun] (to ask workers to protest by refusing to work because of an argument with an employer about pay levels, working conditions, or job losses.)*

The union has called the strike.

The strike was called after the company refused to offer workers a pay rise.

Call an election [Verb + Noun] *(to decide to hold an election in which people vote for someone for a position, especially a political position.)*

The government is planning to call an election before the end of the year.

The prime minister is expected to call an election very soon.

Call attention to someone or something [Verb + Noun] *(to cause people to notice or observe something or someone.)*

I think she dresses like that just to call attention to people.

The poor are calling attention to the issue of unemployment and homelessness.

Call the police [Verb + Noun] *(to telephone an official organization whose job is to make people obey the law and to prevent and solve crime, esp. in an emergency)*

When bob realized his house was robbed, he called the police.

Jane's neighbors called the police when they heard her daughter screams.

Can't afford [Verb + Verb] *(if you can't afford something, you unable to buy it because it's too expensive.)*

The car is too expensive – I can't afford it.

Cathy can't afford the money to go on the trip.

Can't help [Verb + Verb] *(unable to control or stop yourself doing something.)*

Susan can't help smiling even though she knows it's serious.

I couldn't help laughing when I saw that comedy.

Can't stand someone or something [Verb + Verb] *(to hate or dislike someone or something very much.)*

She can't stand bob when he smokes a cigar.

My mother can't stand the loud music.

Jane can't stand her mother-in- law.

Carry weight (with someone) *[Verb + Noun] (to be very influential with someone; to have influence with someone.)*

His argument carried a lot of weight with me.

The witness's testimony carried a lot of weight with the judge.

What he said carried no weight with me.

Cast a spell (on somebody/something) *[Verb + Noun] (to use magic to make something happen to someone; to use magic to change or influence somebody/something.)*

Joe waved her magic wand and cast a spell.

When he looked into her eyes, it felt like she was casting a spell on him.

Cast a vote *[Verb + Noun] (to vote in an election.)*

Anybody over 18 years of age has the right to cast a vote.

The citizens cast their votes for prime minister.

Cast doubt on something *[Verb + Noun] (to make something seem uncertain or less reliable.)*

The new evidence has cast doubt on the accused's innocence.

The fresh information casts doubt on her honesty.

Casual clothes *[Adjective + Noun] (comfortable clothes you choose to wear in your spare time.)*

It's simply a family party, so wearing casual clothes is fine.

Employees are not allowed to wear casual clothes at work.

Casual relationship *[Adjective + Noun] (a relationship that isn't serious and doesn't last a long time.)*

They are just in a casual relationship, but they enjoy each other's company.

We're now just in a casual relationship, but we hope that it will soon become quite serious.

Catch a glimpse of someone/something = catch sight of someone/something *[Verb + Noun] (to see something only for a moment; to see someone or something briefly)*

Jack caught sight of someone with blond hair and knew it was his girlfriend.

Bill caught a glimpse of the robber as he ran out of his house.

Catch a whiff *[Verb + Noun] (to smell something for a moment only; to smell something briefly.)*

I caught a whiff of cigarette when he was talking to me.

John caught a whiff of his girlfriend's perfume as she walked by.

Catch sight of *[Verb + Noun] (to suddenly see someone or something.)*

After catching sight of him in the fitness center, I went over and talked to him.

Last night, I caught sight of him with his girlfriend in the Japanese restaurant.

Cause trouble for someone/something *[Verb + Noun] (to create problems, worries, or difficulties for somebody or something.)*

The floods have been causing trouble all over the village, especially for farmers.

If you let her be with you, she may cause a lot of trouble for you.

Centre of attention *[Noun + Noun] (a person or thing that excites everyone's interest or attention.)*

Helen likes to be the center of attention.

Jane was the centre of attention at her wedding.

Certain amount *[Adjective + Noun] (some, or not very much but more than very little.)*

It will be good for your health if you have a certain amount of red wine every day.

Bill put a certain amount of money in his bank account.

Change course *[Verb + Noun]* *(to start doing something completely new or different; to start moving in a different direction.)*

A lot of students change direction during their first year at college.

The ship didn't change course, and it hit the rocks.

Change your mind *[Verb + Noun]* *(to have a different opinion or intention than you had before; to change a decision or an opinion.)*

At first, I thought he was unreliable and unfriendly, but then I've completely changed my mind.

Alice was about to say something, then she changed her mind.

Claim responsibility for something = take/accept responsibility for something *[Verb + Noun]* *(to say that you're responsible for something bad that has happened.)*

The insurance company refuses to claim responsibility for the damage.

No one has yet claimed responsibility for what happened.

Clean energy *[Adjective + Noun]* *(energy, as electricity or nuclear power, that doesn't pollute or damage environments in its production or use, as opposed to coal and oil.)*

Most clean energy comes from natural sources such as sunlight, wind, rain, tides, etc.

Wind and solar technologies create clean energy, but oil and coal don't.

Close the gap *[Verb + Noun]* *(to reduce the difference between things or groups.)*

Jack is still running second, but he is closing the gap.

The prime minister has been trying to close the gap between rich and poor.

Close together *[Adjective + Adverb]* *(very near to each other.)*

Many couples are sitting close together on the beach.

Our birthdays are close together, so we are going to have a party for the two of us.

Come alive *[Verb + Adverb]* *(become real, lively, active or interesting.)*

The game came alive in the second half after the first goal was scored.

Every New Year's eve, the city comes alive as people come out to celebrate.

The city came alive on New Year's Eve.

Come close (to) *[Verb + Adverb]* *(to nearly/almost do something, reach something, achieve something, complete something, etc.)*

Tom didn't win the game, but he came close.

Jane came close to quitting her job.

We came close to reaching a deal yesterday.

Come to a conclusion *[Verb + Noun]* *(to reach a decision for something after thinking about it.)*

They've come to the conclusion that Susan is not the right person for the job.

They have talked for over 5 hours but yet come to any conclusion.

Come to a realization *[Verb + Noun]* *(to start to understand something; to become aware of something.)*

Peter came to the realization that he was calling the wrong numbers.

After coming to the sudden realization that his house was robbed, he called the police.

Come to a stop *[Verb + Noun]* *(to stop moving or happening)*

Suddenly the dog's barking came to a stop.

The train finally came to a stop so she could get off.

Come to an end [Verb + Noun] *(to finish, of an event, a performance, a meeting, etc.)*

After three hours, the meeting finally came to an end.

The lights will come on as soon as the concert comes to an end.

Come to someone's rescue [Verb + Noun] *(to help someone out of a bad situation; to rescue or save someone or something from danger, failure, or an unpleasant situation.)*

Bill was drowning, but fortunately, his big brother came to his rescue.

Jane was about to drop her new iPhone 7 when her sister came to her rescue.

Come true [Verb + Adjective] *(to become reality; to happen in the way that you have hoped or expected for.)*

I hope your dream will come true.

Bob never thought his dream of owning his own house would come true, but it did.

Comfort food [Noun + Noun] *(the type of food you enjoy very much and often eat when you are feeling sad or worried, often sweet food or food that you liked as a child.)*

Single people have a tendency to eat more comfort foods

Mashed potatoes and gravy is my favorite comfort food.

Commit suicide [Verb + Noun] *(to deliberately kill yourself.)*

Reports suggest that the accused committed suicide.

Jessica is afraid that her boyfriend will commit suicide if she says goodbye to him.

Common knowledge [Adjective + Noun] *(something that almost everyone knows; something that is widely known.)*

It's common knowledge that she is in a relationship.

It is common knowledge that several teachers at that university are incompetent.

Completely different *[Adverb + Adjective]* *(totally different)*

I didn't recognize Cathy after 5 years we had not met. She looks completely different.

The second time he did the research, he got completely different results.

Consider a possibility *[Verb + Noun]* *(to spend time thinking about a possible choice, solution, etc.)*

Have you considered the possibility of studying overseas?

Before deciding to invest your money in stock market, you should consider various possibilities.

Contact details *[Noun + Noun]* *(the information you need to contact someone, such as an email address or a telephone number, etc.)*

May I have your contact details, please?

You can find his contact details on his website.

Cost a fortune *[Verb + Noun]* *(to cost a lot of money)*

It costs a fortune to get the motor car fixed.

A week in a five-star hotel costs a fortune.

Cover costs *[Verb + Noun]* *(to make enough money that is needed to pay for, or do something.)*

I need money to cover the cost of fixing my car.

Their salaries are essential to cover the cost of raising their kids.

Cross someone's mind *[Verb + Noun]* *(if something crosses your mind, you briefly think about it/ you think about it for a short time; to come into your thoughts as a possibility.)*

The thought did cross her mind that her husband might be taking drugs.

The idea of failure never crossed my mind.

It never crossed his mind that Catherine might be lying.

Crystal clear [Noun + Adjective] *(extremely clear or transparent)*

The sky was crystal clear.

The glasses are crystal clear.

After my mother cleaned the windows, they looked crystal clear.

Cut costs [Verb + Noun] *(to reduce the amount that is spent on a service or within an organization.)*

Enterprises tend to cut costs to maximize their profits.

They have to cut costs if they want to avoid bankruptcy.

Cold stare [Adjective + Noun] *(a stare which is unfriendly or lacking normal human feelings.)*

He gave her a cold stare right before he turned away.

She became so frightened when she found that an old man was looking at her with a cold stare.

Connecting flight [Adjective + Noun] *(a connecting flight means that you change from a flight with one number to a flight with another number (possibly a change of airlines).*

We missed the connecting flight to London.

Our connecting flight doesn't leave until 10 o'clock. Now it's just 7:00, so let's find some place to eat first.

Charter flight [Noun + Noun] *(a flight on a plane which is rented by a holiday company for special use such as to transport their customers.)*

We got a really good deal on a charter flight to japan last summer

The charter flight was scheduled to leave at 3:00 p.m.

Catch a glimpse of* = *catch sight of *[Verb + Noun] (to see someone or something for a brief time/ to get a quick look at someone or something.)*

We stopped to catch a glimpse of the mountain.

Tom waited for hours at the airport to catch a glimpse of his favorite singer.

Come into view* = *come into sight *[Verb + Noun] (to move closer so as to become able to be seen.)*

The tallest building of the city came into view as we turned the corner.

The top of the mountain came into view in the distance.

Computer buff *[Noun + Noun] (a person who is proficient at or very knowledgeable about using a computer.)*

Are you a computer buff?

Usually, a computer buff enjoys playing on computers.

Cut and paste *[Verb + Verb] (to move a piece of writing or graphic from one part of a computer file to another place.)*

It's much faster to cut and paste text rather than rewriting it manually.

John hates this job. It's nothing but just cut and paste.

Catch a cold *[Verb + Noun] (to become infected with a cold virus)*

He caught a cold after getting caught in the rain.

Don't go to work if you catch a cold.

Call in sick* = *phone in sick *[Phrase] (to telephone somebody at your place of work to tell them you're not coming to work because you're ill.)*

Peter called in sick and went to see a doctor.

Jane didn't feel well, so she called in sick yesterday.

Catch the latest movie *[Verb + Noun] (to watch a movie that's just come out.)*

Carol loves to dine out with her family and catch the latest movie at the cinema.

Would you like to hang out at the mall and catch the latest movie at the cinema?

Come highly recommended [Phrase] *(to be praised by a lot of people/ to have an excellent reputation.)*

This new coffee shop comes highly recommended.

This movie comes highly recommended by those who have watched it.

Couldn't put something down [Verb + Noun] *(if you couldn't put a book or a novel down, you weren't able to stop reading it until you reached the end since you found it extremely interesting.)*

The novel was so exciting that I couldn't put it down.

The book was extremely interesting. I couldn't put it down until I finished it.

Casual clothes [Adjective + Noun] *(clothes that are comfortable, and suitable for wearing in not formal situations.)*

Our company allows employees to wear casual clothes to work.

I prefer wearing casual clothes rather than wearing formal clothes.

Classic style [Adjective + Noun] *(a very simple style of clothes, furniture etc. That is beautiful and always fashionable.)*

I'm interested in the classic style of clothes as they are timeless.

The classic style of furniture made from solid hardwood will be a great option for your living room.

Cold call [Adjective + Noun] *(an unexpected telephone call made directly to a potential customer to sell something.)*

He got a cold call during a lunch break from someone trying to sell cars.

When I got a cold call, I just said "no, thank."

Cash flow *[Noun + Noun] (the total amount of money moving into and out of a business.)*

We are trying to limit our negative cash flow so that we are not losing too much.

His company ran into cash flow problems and faced liquidation.

Close-cropped hair *[Adjective + Noun] (very short hair.)*

His close-cropped hair makes him look younger.

Robert appeared in a dark suit and tie with his close-cropped hair.

Chain store *[Noun + Noun] ((one of) a group of stores owned by one company and selling the same lines of goods.)*

We bought these loaves of bread in the chain store across from the street.

A lot of retail food chain stores now have unit pricing programs.

Close down *[Phrase] (to stop doing or close a business permanently.)*

Many enterprises have to close down due to high levels of taxation.

The company has closed down its three branches in America.

Catchy tune *[Adjective + Noun] (a song that is pleasing and easily remembered.)*

It was a song with a catchy tune.

I love the catchy tune in that short video.

Classical music *[Adjective + Noun] (music that is developed from a European tradition mainly in the 18th and 19th centuries.)*

My girlfriend likes pop music but I prefer classical music.

Classical music is my father's cup of tea.

Carrier bag *[Noun + Noun] (a plastic or paper bag with handles supplied by a shop* *for carrying shopping.)*

He came up to me with a full carrier bag of sweets from that shop.

Please help me carry this carrier bag of items into the aircraft.

Celebrity endorsement *[Noun + Noun] (a form of promoting a particular product or service by using the fame of a well-known person.)*

The use of celebrity endorsement can increase the attention paid to an advert.

Celebrity endorsement has a great influence on consumer's behavior towards a particular product.

Classified ads *[Adjective + Noun] (small advertisements in a magazine or newspaper, usually made by individuals or small companies.)*

People are able to view all the classified ads for free.

He started looking at the classified ads in the newspaper.

Commercial break *[Adjective + Noun] (a short interruption of a radio or television programme during which advertisements are broadcast or shown.)*

John continues his broadcast after the commercial break is finished.

He went to the kitchen to make coffee during the commercial break in a TV programme.

Commercial channel *[Adjective + Noun] (a TV channel that is paid for by people advertising on it.)*

He likes the idea of a commercial channel, 24/7.

There are many advertisement breaks on commercial channels.

When our son was five, we usually watched many children's TV shows on a commercial channel.

Cultivate your knowledge *[Adjective + Noun] (to increase or improve your knowledge.)*

You can cultivate your knowledge in language by yourself.

He would like to cultivate his knowledge of science, so he's read a lot of science books.

Childish handwriting *[Adjective + Noun] (a style of writing that is typical of a child.)*

Her daughter's childish handwriting really grates on her.

My son began a diary with his childish handwriting.

Cash payment *[Noun + Noun] (an amount of money that you pay by using money in the form of notes and coins.)*

They required us to make a cash payment for our reservation.

We had to make a cash payment for the tickets.

Commercial bank *[Adjective + Noun] (a type of financial institution that provides various financial services, such as accepting deposits and issuing short-term commercial loans.)*

The commercial bank issued me a loan of $50,000 for 4 years to buy a car.

I wasn't charged a fee when I opened a commercial bank current account for cash deposits.

Community service *[Noun + Noun] (work without payment that someone does to help people in their local community.)*

He was sentenced to 150 hours of community service for his crime.

Many people applied to do community service instead of a fine.

He registered to do community service in his area.

Cheesy smile *[Adjective + Noun] (a smile which is very obvious but looks false or not sincere.)*

She snapped a cheesy smile at him.

He flashed a cheesy smile at me before he looks down at his notes.

Canned food = tinned food *[Adjective + Noun] (food that has been preserved in a metal container without air.)*

He doesn't like canned food.

We have had nothing but canned food for two days.

Some tinned food contains lots of preservatives.

Convenience food *[Noun + Noun] (food that is frozen, dried, or canned and can be heated or prepared very quickly and easily.)*

I rely on convenience food from time to time.

Frozen pizza is a popular type of convenience food.

Cement a friendship *[Verb + Noun] (to strengthen a friendship.)*

We'll try our best to cement a friendship that will endure throughout the ages.

Going on holidays together is one of the greatest ways to cement a friendship.

Chronic disease *[Adjective + Noun] (a disease that persists for a long period, and generally cannot be prevented by vaccines or cured by medication.)*

She was diagnosed with a chronic disease.

Her grandfather suffered from a chronic disease.

Chubby cheeks *[Adjective + Noun] (cheeks that are slightly fat in a pleasant and attractive way.)*

The little girl looks cute with chubby cheeks.

She has lovely chubby cheeks.

Clean-shaven face *[Adjective + Noun] (a face that has the beard and mustache shaved off.)*

Her boyfriend has a clean shaven face.

He is a tall and slim man with a clean-shaven face.

Curly hair [Adjective + Noun] *(hair that's not straight.)*

My daughter has blonde curly hair.

Peter had curly hair when he was little.

Curvy body [Adjective + Noun] *(if you have a curvy body, your waist is smaller than your hips and shoulders.)*

Mary has a great curvy body.

If you want to get a curvy body, you must do exercise regularly.

City dweller [Noun + Noun] *(someone who lives in a city.)*

We are Australian city dwellers.

A lot of city dwellers live in rented apartments.

Cold eyes [Adjective + Noun] *(unfriendly eyes/eyes without being affected by emotions.*

She was staring at him with cold eyes.)

Don't look at me with cold eyes!

Close relatives [Adjective + Noun] *(those like parents, children, brothers or sisters.)*

Peter and Sarah are close relatives.

His wife and my wife are close relatives.

Close-knit family [Adjective + Noun] *(if your family is close-knit, all members support and look after each other.)*

They are a very close-knit family.

He is the eldest son in a very close-knit family.

Close friend [Adjective + Noun] *(someone who you can share everything with, who is always there for you, and makes you feel comfortable without fear of judgment.)*

Tom and Mary are close friends.

Sarah and Joe are such close friends that they can almost read each other's minds.

Childhood friend *[Adjective + Noun]* *(someone who has been your friend since you were a child.)*

Jack is a childhood friend of mine.

Alice and Lucy are close childhood friends.

Casual acquaintance *[Adjective + Noun]* *(someone you know a little, not intimately.)*

I was a casual acquaintance of her family in Tokyo.

Tom considered Mary as a casual acquaintance, but he didn't know her well.

Cramped room *[Adjective + Noun]* *(a room that does not have enough space for the people in it.)*

He wants to move out of this cramped room as soon as he can.

This is a cramped room which can hold only ten people.

Comply with the regulations *[Verb + Noun]* *(to obey a set of rules or law/ to do what you have to do or are asked to do.)*

All employees must comply with the regulations.

Businesses must comply with the regulations of safety procedures.

Climate change *[Noun + Noun]* *(a change in global or regional climate patterns, including changes in temperature, wind patterns, and rainfall.)*

Climate change is a global problem that affects people's lives.

The animals are facing the threat of global climate change.

Climate change could affect the habitats of animals and plants.

Check-in desk *[Noun + Noun]* *(the place at the airport where you have your ticket* *checked and deposit your luggage (bags and cases).)*

You must show your passport at the check-in desk.

Do you know where the check-in desk for Singapore airlines is?

Change the subject *[Verb + Noun] (to start a different topic of conversation to avoid embarrassment or distress.)*

Mark felt himself begin to blush and quickly changed the subject.

Our boss began changing the subject when an employee asked him about a pay rise.

Come to an end *[Phrase] (to finish.)*

The holiday has come to an end too soon.

Tom enjoys his math class very much, but it's about to come to an end.

Come to a decision *[Verb + Noun] (to make a choice after thinking carefully.)*

It's time for you to come to a decision on this matter.

Have you come to a decision about what to do next by tomorrow?

Create a good impression *[Verb + Noun] (to make a good impression.)*

The model created a good impression wherever she went.

She created a good impression by helping me with my Spanish.

He created a good impression among the customers.

Create a bad impression *[Verb + Noun] (to make a bad impression.)*

His rude behavior created a bad impression.

Her poor appearance created a bad impression.

COLLOCATIONS/D

Drug trafficking *[Noun + Noun] (the crime of trading in illegal drugs.)*

He was convicted of drug trafficking in the state.

The man who was charged with drug trafficking in Hong Kong faces a severe penalty.

Do-it-yourself book *[Adjective + Noun] (a book that is designed to be done by an amateur at home or as a hobby.)*

His first do-it-yourself book was written in 2005.

It is a really complete do-it-yourself book.

Dead-end job *[Adjective + Noun] (a job that has no prospects of promotion.)*

She was stuck in a dead-end job for nearly 6 years.

Custodial work and waitressing are definitely dead-end jobs.

Distance learning *[Noun + Noun] (a method of study in which students study mostly at home, receiving and sending work to their teachers by post or email.)*

Many students would prefer to take distance-learning courses by computer.

A distance learning course is a perfect way to learn Japanese language.

Desperately worried *[Adverb + Adjective] (feeling extremely worried and nervous.)*

She is desperately worried about her daughter at the moment.

His parents are desperately worried about his safety.

Do an exam = sit an exam = take an exam *[Verb + Noun]*

I am going to do/sit/take an exam in math at the end of this semester.

He usually feels a bit nervous before he takes/sits an exam.

Do someone's duty *[Verb + Noun]* *(do what someone should do at work, at home, or for the community)*

He was doing his duty at work when his boss called.

He was doing his duty as a police officer to prevent crime.

Do the shopping *[Verb + Noun]* *(to buy food and groceries)*

Alice does the shopping every Saturday.

My sister usually does the shopping at our local supermarket.

Deeply ashamed *[Adverb + Adjective]* *(feeling extremely guilty or embarrassed about something you have done or because of something you have done.)*

Smith was deeply ashamed of his behavior at the party.

He felt deeply ashamed of himself for making such a fuss.

Susan was deeply ashamed to admit to her mistake.

Deeply concerned *[Adverb + Adjective]* *(extremely worried about something.)*

She is deeply concerned about/for her father's health.

David was deeply concerned that jane might tell his girlfriend about his bad story.

Deeply shocked *[Adverb + Adjective]* *(feeling very upset or surprised by something bad that happens unexpectedly.)*

They were deeply shocked to hear of their mother's sudden death.

Alice was deeply shocked to discover that she had no money left in her account.

Deeply committed *[Adverb + Adjective]* *(strongly willing to work hard and give your energy and time to something; believing strongly in something.)*

He is a deeply committed teacher.

They are deeply committed to reducing unemployment.

Deeply moved *[Adverb + Adjective] (having strong feelings of sadness or sympathy.)*

We were deeply moved by his plight of the homeless.

He was too moved when Jennifer told him about her mother's death.

Deeply affected *[Adverb + Verb] (to cause somebody strong feelings of sadness, pity, etc.)*

We were deeply affected by the news of his death.

The audience was deeply affected by his speech.

Deeply hurt (of feelings) *[Adverb + Adjective] (very upset or unhappy by something that someone has said or done.)*

Jack felt deeply hurt by what his girlfriend said.

She felt deeply hurt by his refusal to help.

He was deeply hurt by the news.

Deeply care *[Adverb + Verb] (to think that something is very important and worth worrying about.)*

The government should deeply care about environmental issues.

They deeply care about educating their children in the best way possible.

Deeply unhappy *[Adverb + Adjective] (not very happy; very sad)*

Danny was deeply unhappy about his decision.

They were deeply unhappy with the service.

Do a deal *[Verb + Noun] (to complete a negotiation, a mutual arrangement or a transaction, esp. in business, on particular conditions for buying or doing something)*

They have done a deal with France on wine imports.

We are doing a deal with our distributor in Asia next month.

Do a favor *[Verb + Noun] (do something in order to help somebody)*

Could you do me a favor?

Would you please do me a favor and pick up Helen from school today?

Do better *[verb + adverb] (to improve in performance or condition so that it will be more satisfactory, suitable, pleasant, effective, successful etc.)*

Although our team didn't play well today, but I believe that we will do better next time.

"Did you know why everyone else did better than you in the exams?" The teacher asks his student.

Do business (with) *[Verb + Noun] (to engage in business activity of making, buying, selling or supplying goods or services for money).*

It's my pleasure to do business with him.

My brother does a lot of business with overseas customers.

It's not easy to do business in the US if you don't speak English.

Do damage *[Verb + Noun] (to cause physical harm to something so that it is broken, spoiled, injured, less attractive, useful or valuable, etc.)*

Strong winds did a lot of serious damage to the roofs.

The storm did a lot of damage to farmers' crops.

Stop smoking or it can do a lot of damage to your lungs.

Do harm *[Verb + Noun] (to have a bad effect on somebody or something)*

The court case did serious harm to his business.

Drinking too much alcohol can do harm to your liver.

Do good *[Verb + Noun] (to have a good or useful effect on somebody or something)*

It'll do you good if you regularly go for a walk in the morning.

The president didn't do his country much good.

Do likewise *[verb + adverb]* *(do the same thing)*

I am trying to keep the house clean and tidy, and I'd like you to do likewise.

My brother plays guitar very well. I try to do likewise him, but I cannot.

Do the ironing *[Verb + Noun]* *(to make clothes, sheets, etc. smooth with an iron)*

I'll clean the bathroom if you do the ironing.

He likes listening to pop music while he is doing the ironing.

Do the shopping = go shopping *[Verb + Noun]* *(to spend time going to shops/stores and looking for things to buy)*

My sisters and my mother usually do the shopping at our local supermarket.

We are planning to go shopping tonight.

Do well *[verb + adverb]* *(to perform well in a job, a game, an exam, etc.; to be successful)*

I hope Jane will do well in the job interview tomorrow.

Peter is doing very well at school.

Mark did very well in the final exam.

Do work *[Verb + Noun]* *(to put effort into a task or a job)*

John did most of the work yesterday, so he didn't have much work to do today.

He hasn't done enough work for one day. He's going home late.

Do your best *[Verb + Noun]* *(to try as hard as you can to achieve something)*

He is not sure if he can win this game, but he'll do his best.

Do your best if you want to win the race.

Do your duty *[Verb + Noun]* *(do what you should do at work, at home, or for your community; do something that you feel you have to do because it is your moral or legal* responsibility)

I have to do my duty at work today.

He was doing his duty at work when his boss called.

Do exercises *[Verb + Noun] (do physical activity to make your body strong and healthy.)*

I do stomach exercises every morning.

You should do exercises regularly.

Do homework *[Verb + Noun] (to do work that is given by teachers for students to do at home.)*

I'm going to do my homework after dinner.

I'm very busy now. I have to do a lot of homework by 10 o'clock.

Daily life *[Adjective + Noun] (all the things/ activities that you do every day as part of your normal life.)*

Travelling is a great way to escape the routines of our daily life.

Surfing the internet has become part of my daily life.

Dead ahead *[Adverb + Adverb] (straight ahead; directly ahead.)*

According to the map, the fitness center is dead ahead.

The shopping mall is dead ahead. Keep going and you will see it on the right-hand side.

Dead body *[Adjective + Noun] (corpse, or the body of a dead person)*

The police found a dead body in the building.

Surprisingly, the young man's dead body was found in the forest.

Dead end *[Adjective + Noun] (a situation in which no further progress seems possible; a road, street or passage that is closed at one end, and does not lead anywhere.)*

Don't go that way. It is a dead-end street.

He is bored with working that dead-end job with low wages and no hope of promotion.

Dead tired *[Adverb + Adjective]* *(completely exhausted or fatigued; extremely tired.)*

Tom was dead tired after working continuously 14 hours since this morning.

I was dead tired, so I had an early night.

Deadly weapon *[Adjective + Noun]* *(any weapon that's used for killing, including guns, knives, etc.)*

He was carrying a deadly weapon.

He was charged with carrying a deadly weapon.

Declare war *[Verb + Noun]* *(to officially announce the start of a war against another country.)*

The allies officially declared war when Poland was invaded.

The United States declared war on japan in December 1941.

Deeply divided *[Adverb + Adjective]* *(seriously split by disputes or disagreements among the people in a group, organization, or country.)*

Public opinion on gay marriage is deeply divided in lots of countries.

The country is deeply divided by educational and economic opportunities, culture and race.

Deliver a baby *[Verb + Noun]* *(to help or assist a woman in the birth of a baby.)*

The baby was delivered without any problems.

Lucy delivered her second child at home.

Departure time *[Noun + Noun]* *(the time at which a train, bus, aircraft, etc. Is scheduled to depart from a given point of origin.)*

The departure time has changed because of bad weather.

The departure time of this flight is 10.20.

Desk job *[Noun + Noun] (a job that someone does at a desk in an office.)*

Jane's mother would like her to get a desk job.

Mark prefers an outdoor life, so he will not get a desk job.

Detailed description *[Adjective + Noun] (a description that includes a lot of information with many details.)*

Mary gave the police a detailed description of the robber.

She gave us a very detailed description of john's appearance.

The police need him to provide them with a detailed description of the situation.

Diametrically opposed *[Adverb + Adjective] (completely different from each other.)*

They hold diametrically opposed points of view on most political issues.

We hold diametrically opposed views on most political issues.

Our viewpoints are diametrically opposed.

Direct flight *[Adjective + Noun] (a flight that does not stop on its way to a destination.)*

There are many direct flights to Canada.

There weren't any direct flights to Los Angeles yesterday.

Directly opposite *[Adverb + Adjective] (straight across from or on the other side of someone or something)*

Jessica's house is directly opposite the church.

We found a movie theater directly opposite the Japanese restaurant.

Dirty joke *[Adjective + Noun] (a joke that's indelicate or related to sex.)*

Please don't tell any dirty jokes at my wedding, peter.

The guys in the pub told many dirty jokes.

Dirty player *[Adjective + Noun] (a player who behaves dishonestly, especially by cheating in a game.)*

Jack was a dirty player.

David is not a dirty player although he loses his temper from time to time.

Distant relative *[Adjective + Noun] (a relative related to you but not closely.)*

I have got some distant relatives in Canada, but I don't even know their names.

Jane is his distant relative.

Do a favour *[Verb + Noun] (to do something to help someone as an act of kindness.)*

Would you please do me a favor and take my son to the school?

My brother did me a favour by lending me his car.

Doesn't matter *[Verb + Verb]* never mind.

It doesn't matter if you are late. It's just a formal party.

It doesn't really matter whether we win or lose the game. We just play it for fun.

Don't care = don't mind *[Verb + Verb] (to not be concerned about something; it doesn't matter to someone.)*

John doesn't care if he loses his job. He doesn't like it anyway.

His wife got upset when people insulted him, but he didn't care.

Drive someone crazy = drive someone insane = drive someone mad *[Phrase] (to make somebody feel very annoyed or upset; to irritate someone.)*

The dog's constant barking drove him crazy.

Her children always drive her crazy when they are tired and in a bad mood.

Drop the subject = drop it *[Verb + Noun] (to stop talking about something, especially because it is annoying or upsetting.)*

Honestly, I don't want to talk about sex anymore - let's drop the subject.

If you don't want to talk about it, let's drop the subject.

Joe wished her mother would just drop the subject.

Dual nationality *[Adjective + Noun] (the state of being a citizen of two different countries concurrently.)*

Paul has dual Canadian and American nationality.

There is an increasing number of people who have dual nationality these days.

Desperately lonely *[Adverb + Adjective] (very unhappy since you are alone or you have no friends.)*

I felt desperately lonely for the first few months in Scotland.

At first, Sarah felt desperately lonely when she was at school.

Day trip *[Noun + Noun] (a visit to a place in which you go there and then return home on the same day, usually for pleasure.)*

Last week, my family had a day trip to the beach.

I suggest we take a day trip to France next Saturday.

Domestic flights *[Noun + Noun] (a flight that begins and ends inside a country.)*

Smoking is not allowed on all domestic flights.

Domestic flights are often cheaper than international ones

We arrived at the airport one hour ahead of time for the domestic flight.

Dramatic setting *[Adjective + Noun]* *(a set of surroundings which is exciting and impressive.)*

The festival took place in a dramatic setting near Bamburgh castle.

Most men choose a dramatic setting for their first date.

Dense forest = thick forest *[Adjective + Noun]* *(forest that is packed tightly together with trees.)*

The man who lives near the dense forest with his wife is a poor woodcutter.

There is a path through the dense forest

Departure lounge *[Noun + Noun]* *(a large room in an airport where you sit and wait before getting onto an aircraft.)*

All passengers must go through passport control before getting into the departure lounge.

We played cards to kill time when we were waiting for our flight in the departure lounge.

Drift apart *[Phrase]* *(to become less intimate or friendly and gradually end a relationship with someone.)*

My roommates in college and I have drifted apart over the years.

We were close friends at high school, but when we went to different colleges, we just drifted apart.

Desktop PC = desktop computer *[Noun + Noun]* *(a personal computer that fits on top of a desk and isn't moved easily.)*

I prefer a desktop computer rather than a laptop.

John has just bought a desktop PC. He is going to use it for writing long essays and editing photos.

Detached house *[Adjective + Noun]* *(a house that stands alone, not connected to any other house.)*

He owns a large detached house which is surrounded by a garden.

The price of the detached house is so expensive that she can't afford it.

Do up (a property) [Verb + Noun] *(to repair or decorate an old building so that it is in a better condition.)*

He is going to do up his run-down house.

I need to do up my own house. It's very old now.

Dream home [Noun + Noun] *(a home that is the best you can imagine.)*

Her dream home is large and spacious.

What is your dream home like?

Do market research [Verb + Noun] *(the activity of gathering information about target markets, consumers' needs and preferences.)*

We are business owners – we do market research every day.

We use online tools to do market research.

Drum up business [Verb + Noun] *(to try to find new customers and increase business activity.)*

He tried to drum up business by introducing himself to potential clients who have not heard of him before.

We are using the event to drum up business for our new investment company.

Dress up to the nines [Phrase] *(to put on extremely fashionable or formal clothes for a special occasion.)*

Mary always dresses up to the nines whenever she goes to parties or weddings.

Peter is going to dress to the nines tomorrow because he is meeting his girlfriend's parents for the first time.

Do a job-share [Verb + Noun] *(a situation in which two or more part-time workers* *share equal parts of the same work.)*

My wife did a job-share with another woman who had a small child.

She is considering trying to do a job-share with a friend in a boutique.

Droopy moustache *[Adjective + Noun] (moustache that is long and hanging down heavily.)*

The old man had a big droopy moustache.

Her father has gentle blue eyes and a long droopy moustache.

Distant relatives *[Adjective + Noun] (those like the children of a cousin of your father or mother.)*

Some of my distant relatives live in New York.

All his close and distant relatives came to the wedding.

Dysfunctional family *[Adjective + Noun] (a family in which the relationships between children and parents are strained and unnatural.)*

She dislikes spending holidays with her boyfriend's dysfunctional family.

Her husband's behaviour resulted from growing up in an extremely dysfunctional family.

Do up an old house *[Verb + Noun] (to repair, paint, and improve an old house.)*

We are starting to do up an old house.

He intends to do up an old house and turn it into a hotel.

Do research = do a research project = carry out a research project = conduct a research project *[Verb + Noun] (to make a detailed study of something in order to discover new information or new facts.)*

Where can I do research to find answers for grammar homework?

He loves science, so he does research on it and writes about it.

London is one of the best places to carry out a research project.

***Do a course* = take a course** *[Verb + Noun]* *(to enroll in a course.)*

Tom has decided to do/take a course in art and design.

Peter said that he wanted to do a course in computing.

***Do a degree/diploma* = study for a degree = take a degree** *[Verb + Noun] (to study to obtain a qualification after completing a university or college course.)*

My sister wants to do/take a degree in journalism.

I think he has the personal skills needed to do a degree in law.

Do an essay/assignment *[Verb + Noun] (to write an essay/assignment.)*

She always does an essay plan before she starts writing.

I'm very busy now. I have to do an assignment.

***Do a lecture/talk* = give a lecture** *[Verb + Noun] (to teach a group of people about a particular subject, especially at a college or university.)*

He will be doing a lecture at Harvard University tomorrow.

The professor agreed to give a lecture about global development.

Donate money (to) *[Verb + Noun] (to give money to an organization, especially to a school, hospital, or charity.)*

Many big corporations donate money to the local orphanage.

Our company has donated a lot of money to people who suffer from cancers.

Devastating floods *[Adjective + Noun] (floods that a lot of harm or damage.)*

The village was struck by devastating floods last summer.

Three bridges are being rebuilt after the devastating floods of September.

Draw to a close *[Phrase] (to come to an end/ to finish; to end.)*

The summer vacation is drawing to a close.

As the party drew to a close, peter thanked everyone for coming.

Do one's best = try one's best _[Verb + Noun]_ _(to do or perform as well as you can.)_

Tom did his best to pass the exam.

I did my best to carry out the plan.

Mary did her best to explain what had happened.

Needless to say = it goes without saying that _[Phrase]_ _(obviously.)_

Needless to say, she didn't believe him.

Needless to say, he was so excited about the journey.

It goes without saying that they are very happy about the new baby.

It goes without saying that he will be paid for the extra hours he works.

COLLOCATIONS/E

Enhance the level of job performance *[Phrase]*

A vast amount of work experience will allow him to enhance the level of job performance.

This rewarding perk will encourage them to try hard and enhance the level of job performance.

Enter into an agreement *[Verb + Noun] (to agree to be part of an official agreement.)*

The parties entered into an agreement in good faith.

We entered into an agreement with a private firm.

Engage someone in conversation *[Verb + Noun] (to start having a conversation with someone.)*

He tried to engage her in conversation.

Tom came close to Mary and fairly engaged her in conversation.

Enhance sb's resume *[Phrase]*

Volunteer work is an effective way to enhance your resume.

Peter wants to enhance his resume by participating in extra-curricular activities.

Ease the pain *[Verb + Noun] (to make free from pain, lessen the pain.)*

These tablets will help you to ease the pain.

He used marijuana to ease the pain.

Early days *[Adjective + Noun] (a time too soon to make a judgment or come to a conclusion about something.)*

His new business is earning a lot of profit, but it's early days.

Our progress has been quite rapid, but it's early days.

Early night [Adjective + Noun] (an occasion when you go to bed earlier than usual, especially when you are tired.)

You've got to get up early tomorrow, so I think you need to have an early night.

I feel exhausted after work, so I think I'd better get an early night

Early riser [Adjective + Noun] (a person who habitually gets up early in the morning.)

My parents are early risers, usually up by 5.30 am.

I was surprised to see my mom asleep at 9:00, normally she is such an early riser.

Early start [Adjective + Noun] (an occasion when you start something or get started on a journey, activity, etc., early in the morning.)

We've got an early start tomorrow, so I think we'd better get some sleep.

They are going a long way, so they want to get an early start tomorrow.

Easy money [Adjective + Noun] (money that's made without working hard, and sometimes dishonestly earned.

The easy money he had made evaporated quickly.

Not everyone can make easy money on the stock market.

Easy target [Adjective + Noun] (someone or something that's easy to attack, criticize, cheat, or steal from.)

The elderly people and children are often easy targets for criminals.

They think she's an easy target because she's a very rich woman.

Eat properly = eat healthily [Verb + Adverb] (to eat proper amounts of food that is good for you.)

A majority of people who live alone tend not to eat properly.

A lot of old people who live alone don't eat properly.

If you don't want to have health problems, you need to eat properly.

Eat well *[Verb + Adverb]* *(to eat a lot of good food.)*

I ate well when I stayed at my uncle's place.

Tom hasn't eaten well recently.

Eating habits = eating patterns *[Verb + Noun]* *(what types of food someone usually eats, in what quantities, and when.)*

She tried to adopt good eating habits by eating a balanced diet.

"You must change your eating habits if you want to be healthy" her mom said.

Economic growth *[Adjective + Noun]* *(steady growth in the productive capacity of the economy, such as an increase in the number of goods and services over a period of time.)*

The rates of economic growth in the developing countries are increasingly steadily.

Rapid economic growth has caused environmental problems in several countries.

Educational game *[Adjective + Noun]* *(a game that helps students to learn as well as amusing them.)*

Educational games are very useful for students.

"Word up" is supposed to be one of the best educational game for English learners.

Eke out a living *[Verb + Noun]* *(to earn just enough money or food to survive.)*

Homeless kids managed to eke out a living by selling drinks to tourists on a beach.

Many street children eke out a living by shining shoes to tourists.

Empty promise [Adjective + Noun] *(a promise that its maker probably won't keep, fulfill or carry out.)*

The salesman makes empty promises so that we will buy his products.

Tom usually makes empty promises to his little sister.

Empty words [Adjective + Noun] *(words that have no meaning in themselves or that won't lead to action.)*

Peter said he'd never smoke cigarettes again, but they were just more empty words.

"I want real actions from you, not more empty words" his boss said.

Enter a plea [Verb + Noun] *(a statement that someone makes in a court of law to say whether they are guilty or not guilty of a crime.)*

The court rejected the plea he entered.

In some cases, a defendant is allowed to refuse to enter a plea.

Enter politics [Verb + Noun] *(to begin the profession of being a politician.)*

John entered politics at the age of 25.

Cheryl entered politics after a career in medicine.

Entry-level job [Adjective + Noun] *(a job at the lowest level of pay or responsibility in a company or organization, normally suitable for unskilled or inexperienced workers.)*

E-commerce is offering college graduates unlimited choices of entry-level jobs.

Peter has got an entry-level job in sales.

Equal rights (for someone) [Adjective + Noun] *(the same rights for everyone regardless of races, genders, classes, etc.)*

Employment law provides equal rights for women.

Equal rights are still being struggled for by women in many parts of the world.

Equally important *[Adverb + Adjective] (to the same importance extent.)*

Exercise regularly and eat a balanced diet are equally important for maintaining good health.

I don't think money and happiness are equally important.

Essential services *[Adjective + Noun] (basic public needs, such as water, electricity, gas, medical care, education, etc. That are often supplied to people's houses.)*

The government provides her children most essential services.

Essential services are extremely important in most countries.

Ethical investment *[Adjective + Noun] (the practice of investing in companies whose activities or products are not considered harmful to society or the environment.)*

Ethical investment is changing the way that companies work.

It will not be an ethical investment if we buy shares in an enterprise that exploits workers in poor countries.

Ethical standards *[Adjective + Noun] (principles that generate trust, good behavior, fairness, and kindness, which typically occur in a company, or an organization.)*

Nowadays, ethical standards are often considered as less important than profits in business.

People might not face health problems if the food industry has ethical standards.

Ethnic minority *[Adjective + Noun] (a group of people living in a country or area in which most people have a different culture and different traditions.)*

Discrimination against ethnic minorities is prohibited by law in most countries.

The populations of ethnic minorities have increased significantly over the period of 10 years.

Even number *[Adjective + Noun] (any number (any integer) that can be exactly divided by 2, such as 2, 4, 6, 8 etc.)*

-16, 4, 8 and 32 are all even numbers, but 1, 3 and 5 are odd numbers.

Jane always thinks even numbers are lucky when she buys lottery tickets.

Evenly matched *[Adverb + Verb]* *(if two opponents are evenly matched, each person has an equal chance to win; equal in skill or ability.)*

The two boxers are fairly evenly matched.

The two football teams remain evenly balanced.

Every single *[Adverb + Adjective]* *(all of them (used for emphasis))*

We need to know every single detail of her life.

There is no milk left. My greedy brother drank every single one!

Exactly the same *[Phrase]* *(identical; accurately, precisely, or exactly the one or ones referred to or mentioned.)*

This vacuum cleaner works in exactly the same way as the other.

Susan was wearing exactly the same dress as her sister was.

Exceed (someone's) expectations *[Verb + Noun]* *(to be much bigger, greater or better than expected.)*

This year, our company's net profits have exceeded all expectations.

His performance exceeded all his friends' expectations.

Express concern *[Verb + Noun]* *(to show a feeling of worry about something.)*

Many people expressed a lot of concern over the proposed changes in the law.

She has expressed concern about the state of her father's health.

Express (an) interest (in) = show (an) interest (in) *[Verb + Noun]* *(to show a feeling that you're interested in something, want to know about or take part in something.)*

A Japanese investor has expressed a genuine interest in the project.

Many buyers have shown an interest in the deal.

An Indian investor has expressed a lot of interest in our proposal.

Extend a deadline *[Verb + Noun] (to give somebody more time to do something.)*

They have agreed to extend the deadline for completing the school.

The teacher agreed to extend the deadline for completion of his essay.

Elderly person *[Adjective + Noun] (someone who is old.)*

An elderly person wanted me to give him a hand.

He was arrested for stealing money from an elderly person.

Enjoy someone's company *[Noun + Noun] (to enjoy being or spending time with someone/ to get on really well with someone.)*

I always love my girlfriend and enjoy her company.

Tom and Mary are always together, they absolutely enjoy each other's company.

Eat a balanced diet *[Verb + Noun] (to eat the proper quantities and proportions of foods required for healthy growth and activity.)*

Eating a well-balanced diet is essential for good health.

It's important for us to eat a healthy, balanced diet.

Eat like a horse *[Verb + Noun] (to eat a lot/ to eat large amounts of food.)*

No wonder he's so fat. He eats like a horse. John works like a horse and eats like a horse, so he never gets fat.

Jane's so thin even though she eats like a horse.

My mom always cooks a lot of food when my friends and I come for lunch because we eat like horses.

Endangered species *[Adjective + Noun] (a species of animal or plant that is seriously at risk of extinction due to human activities or changes in climate.)*

Wolves and elephants are endangered species.

The number of endangered species in our country is increasing almost every day.

Environmentally friendly *[Adverb + Adjective] (not harmful to the environment.)*

Local businesses are encouraged to produce environmentally friendly products.

Cycling is not only good for people's health but also very environmentally friendly.

Most organic products are environmentally friendly.

Exhaust fumes *[Noun + Noun] (the toxic gasses produced by an engine as waste products.)*

The air was polluted with the exhaust fumes from numerous automobiles.

The exhaust fumes from trucks and cars could seriously damage people's health.

Emotional intelligence *[Adjective + Noun] (the ability to identify, understand and manage your own emotions or the emotions of others.)*

I like to read books about emotional intelligence.

Emotional intelligence is a wide selection of skills that children should develop.

Earn a living *[Verb + Noun] (to earn money to buy the things you need in life)*

I earn a living as a writer.

He earns a living by selling his paintings.

She earns a living by selling jewelry.

Earn a (good) living *[Verb + Noun] (to work and earn enough money to pay for everything you need.)*

David earns a good living from selling his books.

You have to find a good job if you want to earn a good living.

Extended family *[Adjective + Noun] (a family unit including grandparents, parents, children, aunts, uncles, and other relatives.)*

My brothers and I have been grown up in an extended family.

Most Chinese elderly people live in an extended family, usually with a son or a daughter and grandchildren.

Embark on a career *[Verb + Noun] (to begin a career.)*

My brother embarked on a career as a game developer last year.

Encouraged by her father, Sarah embarked on a career in literature.

Enforce the law *[Verb + Noun] (to punish people who do not obey the law/ to make a law active or effective.)*

Those who enforce the law must obey the law.

Government agencies must enforce the law immediately.

The duty of the police and the court is to enforce the law.

COLLOCATIONS/F

Fall in love *[Verb + Noun] (to start to love someone you're attracted to.)*

They fell passionately in love with each other.

John fell madly in love with a young Japanese girl at first sight.

Firm friend *[Adjective + Noun] (a friend you like a lot and intend to keep.)*

We met five months ago and soon became firm friends.

I'll try my best to remain firm friends for the rest of my life.

Fight for one's life *[Verb + Noun] (to struggle or to make a great effort to survive.)*

His condition is very serious. He is fighting for his life in hospital.

She was in a critical condition after a serious road collision. She is still fighting for her life at present.

Fall behind with your studies *[Verb + Noun] (to make less progress than others/ to fail to keep level with someone.)*

If you miss even just a few classes, you will easily fall behind with your studies.

Tom really fell behind with his studies last semester.

Family gathering *[Noun + Noun] (social occasion including an entire family.)*

We held a large family gathering last week.

Lunar New Year is one of the best times for a family gathering in China.

Fasten your seatbelts *[Verb + Noun] (to close or join together the two parts of your seatbelts to hold you in your seat.)*

Passengers must fasten their seatbelts before landing at the airport.

Ladies and gentlemen, please fasten your seatbelts in preparation for landing.

Fully booked *[Adverb + Verb]* *(if a hotel, restaurant, theater, or transport service is fully booked, it has no tickets, rooms, or tables left for a particular time.)*

The restaurant we liked was fully booked, so we looked for another one nearby.

I'm terribly sorry to say all the rooms are fully booked until 9:00 a.m.

Face a challenge *[Verb + Noun]* *(to be ready to deal with a challenging situation which requires great mental or physical effort.)*

The Chinese investors face the challenge of completing the building on time.

The new president now faces many difficult challenges.

Face the fact(s) *[Verb + Noun]* *(to confront and accept the truth about someone or something, although it is unpleasant.)*

Finally, he had to face the facts.

Julie had to face the facts when her boss told her he didn't like her report. She must rewrite it.

Fail miserably *[Verb + Adverb]* *(to have an amazingly terrible failure; to be highly unsuccessful.)*

That guy failed miserably.

He tried acting, but he failed miserably.

Fair deal *[Adjective + Noun]* *(a reasonable deal or transaction in business.)*

He got a fair deal when he sold his own car.

We always get a fair deal when we book with them.

Fall asleep *[Verb + Adjective]* *(to begin to sleep.)*

Joe fell asleep during the movie.

My mom was so tired that she fell asleep sitting in her chair.

Fall dramatically *[Verb + Adverb] (to fall suddenly.)*

The company's sales have fallen dramatically over the last 3 months.

Share prices have fallen dramatically in trading recently.

False impression = be under the impression (that) *[Adjective + Noun] (something that you believe is true, but actually it is not true.)*

The rumor gave a false impression of his wealth.

Jack was under the impression that you were married.

False teeth *[Adjective + Noun] (artificial teeth; teeth that are unnatural.)*

Her false teeth need replacing because she gets ulcers all the time.

Her false teeth look too white to be real.

Familiar face *[Adjective + Noun] (a person that you know individually.)*

John was glad to see familiar faces when he got to my wedding.

Lucy felt a bit lonely when she didn't see familiar faces at the party.

Far away *[Adverb + Adverb] (a long way away; distant from a particular place.)*

I like to travel to faraway places.

How far away is the hotel?

It's not as far away as the shopping mall.

Fast asleep = sound asleep *[Adverb + Adjective] (sleeping deeply; sleeping in a way that makes it difficult to wake you.)*

I was fast asleep when he called.

John is fast asleep on the sofa.

Fast becoming *[Adverb + Verb] (quickly becoming (over a short period of time).)*

This company is fast becoming a major exporter of red wine.

English is fast becoming important to people all over the world.

Fatal accident *[Adjective + Noun]* *(an accident that causes someone to die.)*

Jane's uncle died in a fatal car accident last week.

That was a fatal road accident.

Fatal mistake *[Adjective + Noun]* *(a very serious mistake that has terrible consequences.)*

Marrying him had been the fatal mistake of her life.

He made a fatal mistake when he invested all his money in a startup company.

Feel guilty *[Verb + Adjective]* *(to feel bad, ashamed and sorry because you have done something wrong.)*

Tom felt so guilty about forgetting his mother's birthday.

John was feeling guilty about having shouted at his girlfriend.

Feel strongly (about) *[Verb + Adverb]* *(to have a very strong, definite or passionate opinion (about something).)*

Mr. Johnson feels strongly that the trial was unfair.

They feel strongly that the gap between the rich and the poor is increasingly widened.

Fight a fire *[Verb + Noun]* *(to try to put out a large fire from burning)*

His neighbors and fire crews had to fight a large fire in his house last night.

Fighting a fire is a dangerous thing to do.

Figure prominently *[Verb + Adverb]* *(to be an important part of something, such as a process, an event, a story, etc.)*

His attendance figured prominently at my wedding.

The issues of gas import and export will figure prominently in the next election.

Fill a gap *[Verb + Noun] (to provide something that is missing or needed)*

After filling a gap in the market, their products do well.

To fill the gap, we must recruit a new employee.

Fill in a form *[Verb + Noun] (to complete a form by writing the necessary information in the spaces.)*

I took an application form and filled it in.

You can find and fill in an order form on my website.

Flood of tears *[Noun + Noun] (if someone was in a flood of tears, he/she was crying a lot.)*

They were in floods of tears when they said goodbye to each other.

The little boy was in a flood of tears when he came home.

Fall into ruin *[Verb + Noun] (if something falls into ruin, it gets damaged or destroyed.)*

A large white house had been left to fall into ruin.

Don't let your house fall into ruin.

Fast-flowing river *[Adjective + Noun] (a river which is flowing rapidly.)*

He found it difficult to swim across the fast-flowing river.

Swimming in a fast flowing river is very dangerous.

Far-off destination *[Adjective + Noun] (a place which is far away from you/ somewhere a long distance away.)*

We are flying to some far-off destination next month.

I would like to travel to some far-off destination to explore new places on the earth.

Fall for someone *[Phrase]* *(to be or fall in love with someone/ to become infatuated with someone.)*

Jack is smart and good-looking; all the women fall for him.

Lucy's gorgeous! At the first time bill saw her at the restaurant, he fell for her immediately.

Fall head over heels in love *[Phrase]* *(to start to love somebody very much, especially suddenly.)*

Richard fell head over heels in love with his new girlfriend.

John fell head over heels in love with Rosie, and they were married within the year.

Fall out with *[Phrase]* *(to have an argument or disagreement with someone about something and stop being friendly with him/her.)*

Jane and her brother used to fall out a lot.

Bill fell out with his parents after he told them he was gay.

Follow a recipe *[Verb + Noun]* *(to prepare and cook a particular type of food by following a set of instructions.)*

Do you usually follow a recipe while cooking?

When my mom makes pancakes, she doesn't need to follow a recipe.

Foot the bill *[Verb + Noun]* *(to pay the bill/ to pay for something.)*

You paid for lunch yesterday. Let me foot the bill for dinner today.

Her parents footed the bill for her MBA education.

Fussy eater *[Adjective + Noun]* *(someone who is not easily satisfied or has very high standards about what to eat.)*

My daughter is a fussy eater who never eats meat or vegetables.

Don't worry about my father – he is not a fussy eater.

Flick through something *[Verb + Noun] (to turn quickly through the pages of a book, magazine, newspaper etc.)*

She flicked through the magazine without reading any page for more than a few seconds.

I decided to buy the book although I didn't flick through it.

First-time buyer *[Adjective + Noun] (a person who is buying a house or an apartment for the first time, especially by borrowing money from a bank.)*

Peter made a lot of questions because he was a first-time buyer.

Being a first-time buyer is a bit tricky.

Fully furnished *[Adverb + Adjective] (if a house, flat, or room is fully furnished, it is available to be rented with all furniture already in it.)*

The apartment is fully furnished and has a balcony overlooking the river.

The house that I rented in Sydney was fully furnished.

Fashion house *[Noun + Noun] (a company that designs and sells new styles of expensive clothes, shoes, bags, etc.)*

She was wearing a brand-new dress designed by a fashion house in Paris.

Susan works for a well-known fashion house in great Portland Street.

Fashion icon *[Noun + Noun] (someone who is well-known as being highly fashionable.)*

Diana is my most admired fashion icon.

She was the most influential fashion icon of the 20th century.

Fashion show *[Noun + Noun] (an event at which fashion models show new styles of clothes to the public.)*

Sarah modeled at a fashion show in Paris.

We are planning to attend a fashion show in spring.

Fashionable boutiques *[Adjective + Noun]* (a small shop that sells fashionable clothes.)

I bought clothes in that fashionable boutiques.

The street is popular with its fashionable boutiques.

Flash flood *[Noun + Noun]* (a sudden and severe flood, usually caused by heavy rain.)

We must hurry up or we'll get caught in a flash flood.

Do you see any possibility of a flash flood?

Freezing cold *[Adverb + Adjective]* (very cold/ extremely cold.)

It's been freezing cold recently.

My hands are freezing cold!

It's freezing cold outside.

Flash flood *[Adjective + Noun]* (a flood of great volume that happens suddenly, usually due to heavy rain.)

A lot of people were drowned in the flash floods.

The severe thunderstorm caused flash floods in several mountainous areas.

Face financial difficulties *[Verb + Noun]* (if you face financial difficulties, you have to deal with problems in finance.)

His business began to face financial difficulties in 2002-03.

The company may face financial difficulties for a couple of months.

Single parents tend to face financial difficulties.

Food shortage *[Noun + Noun]* (a situation in which there is a lack of food that people need.)

Several countries in Africa are suffering from a food shortage.

The food shortage happened due to drought and war.

Fat-free food *[Adjective + Noun] (food that contains no fat.)*

She wakes up at 5:30, goes jogging and eats only fat-free food.

Exercising and eating fat-free food products will help people to lose weight.

Food additives *[Noun + Noun] (artificial substances added to food to enhance its flavor or colour or to preserve it.)*

Some manufacturers regard food additives as being beneficial.

White crystalline compound and nitrite are used as food additives to enhance flavor.

Food preservatives *[Noun + Noun] (substances added to a processed food for humans in order to protect against decay, discoloration, or spoilage.)*

A lot of customers are pleased to buy goods with food preservatives.

Manufacturers use food preservatives to maintain the freshness of food.

Fresh food *[Adjective + Noun] (food that has been recently produced, picked, caught, or prepared.)*

She enjoys fresh food.

It is difficult to buy cheap and good-quality fresh food in an urban area.

Frozen food *[Adjective + Noun] (food that has been preserved by freezing and kept frozen until used.)*

Frozen food is made good use by many housewives.

Frozen food is frozen in the freezer.

Fatal disease = deadly disease *[Adjective + Noun] (an illness that causes death.)*

Aids is a fatal disease.

She contracted a fatal disease while travelling in Europe.

Fair-minded person *[Adjective + Noun]* *(a person who is just and impartial (treats everyone equally).*

He is the most fair-minded person I've ever known.

Her father was a very fair-minded employer.

Friendly smile *[Adjective + Noun] (a kind and pleasant smile.)*

Sarah gave tom a friendly smile.

The receptionist greeted us a warm and friendly smile.

Flowing hair *[Adjective + Noun] (hair that is long and hangs down freely.)*

Alice has long black flowing hair.

She looks beautiful with long flowing hair.

Foreign/international/overseas travel *[Adjective + Noun] (the activity of travelling abroad (outside your country).)*

He enjoys foreign travel and goes away every chance that he gets.

Overseas travel never really appealed to her until she retired.

International travel has expanded my international view.

Fair hair *[Adjective + Noun] (hair is blonde (=light yellow) or very light brown in colour.)*

She has big blue eyes and fair hair.

Mary is a pretty girl with long curly fair hair.

Fully-fitted kitchen *[Adjective + Noun] (a kitchen fitted with appliances and units such as a dishwasher, a washing machine, a fridge freezer, an oven, etc.)*

The flat is very modern with a fully-fitted kitchen featuring a refrigerator and a microwave.

The apartment is elegantly decorated, with a fully-fitted kitchen and new bathroom with a shower.

Feel homesick *[Verb + Adjective]* *(if you feel homesick, you feel sad and alone because you are far from home.)*

I felt homesick when I was away from my home.

The first time he felt homesick when he was living in Melbourne.

Feel at home *[Phrase]* *(to feel comfortable and relaxed as if you were in your home.)*

Jane liked her dormitory room. She really felt at home there.

They did whatever they could to make us feel at home.

By the end of the first week, tom was beginning to feel at home in his new job.

Fair trial *[Adjective + Noun]* *(a trial that is conducted fairly or justly.)*

As opposed to the first trial, the second trial was a fair trial.

We don't think it was a fair trial. The young man should have been given a chance to prove himself.

Face the death penalty *[Verb + Noun]* *(to face a sentence or punishment of death, usually for a serious crime such as murder.)*

If convicted, he could face the death penalty.

The murderer faced the death penalty for killing a victim of another race.

COLLOCATIONS/G

Gap year *[Adjective + Noun] (a year between leaving school and starting university that a young person spends working and/or travelling.)*

Jane took a gap year to travel before coming to university.

He took a gap year to work right after high school.

Gentle exercise *[Adjective + Noun] (exercise not involving too much physical effort.)*

I do some gentle exercise as part of my daily routine.

He was recommended to take some gentle exercise every day.

Go wild *[Verb + Adjective] (to behave in a very excited uncontrolled/ to get very angry.)*

The crowd went wild as soon as Cristiano Ronaldo scored a goal.

When he told her what he'd done, she went wild.

Get into an argument *[Verb + Noun] (to enter a quarrel or an angry disagreement with someone about someone or something.)*

She doesn't want to get into an argument with her mom about her dad.

Tom got into an argument about money with his wife.

Jack got into an argument with Bob in the pub last night.

Graduate from university *[Verb + Noun] (to leave university after getting a degree.)*

He graduated from University in May 2002.

Students tend to find work soon after graduating from university.

Gifted children *[Adjective + Noun] (children with an impressive natural ability or intelligence.)*

That is a school for gifted children.

Most gifted children prefer factual writing rather than creative writing.

Go into production [Verb + Noun] *(to begin being made.)*

The car model will go into production later this year.

William Shatner Rivet motorcycle is due to go into production next year.

Grasp the importance of [Verb + Noun] *(to understand how important something is.)*

He failed to grasp the importance of my words.

I grasped the importance of his message.

Give someone a reason [Phrase] *(to give someone a cause or an explanation for something that has happened.)*

He couldn't give her a good reason why he was late.

She gave me a good reason why she didn't answer me yet.

Give an account of something [Phrase] *(to give someone an explanation for something.)*

She was too shocked to give a clear account of the incident.

He was asked to give an account of his actions.

Get the message [Verb + Noun] *(to understand what someone is trying to tell you, although that is not being said directly.)*

She didn't want to see him anymore. Why didn't he get the message?

When she didn't return his phone calls, he finally got the message.

Gain some valuable experience [Phrase] *(to obtain some valuable experience)*

Working and traveling are both great ways for people to gain some valuable experience.

He is looking for an opportunity to gain some valuable experience.

Give someone countless opportunities [Phrase] *(to give a person so many opportunities)*

His English skills are excellent. This gives him countless opportunities to get a scholarship and study overseas.

Reading books give me countless opportunities to learn something new.

Give someone a lift [Phrase] *(to take somebody somewhere in a car or other vehicle.)*

He gave me a lift to the station.

He jumped on the back of my bike and I gave him a lift to the school.

Get divorced [Phrase] *(legally end someone's marriage.)*

Alice's ex-husband and she got divorced two years ago.

Mary has never remarried since they got divorced.

Give someone a call = give someone a ring [Phrase] *(to telephone somebody.)*

I'm too busy to answer your phone now. I'll give you a call later tonight.

If you need any further information, just give me a call.

Go/enter into partnership with someone [Phrase] *(to agree to be a partner in business with someone.)*

David went/entered into partnership with mark to form the firm in 2002.

Jack went/entered into partnership with a local trader who he'd been doing business with.

Go mad [Phrase] *(very angry or annoyed; to start behaving in a dangerous uncontrolled manner.)*

She will go mad when she sees the damage.

He went mad and tried to attack people on the street.

Go bald [Phrase] *(lose your hair (have little or no hair on your head).*

My brother started going bald in his thirties.

David's head is starting to go bald.

Go grey [Phrase] *(if your hair goes grey, it starts to become white.)*

Her hair seems to have gone grey very quickly.

She's gone very grey.

Go blind [Phrase] *(to make someone unable to see.)*

The disease made him go blind.

Doctors think she will go blind.

Go deaf [Phrase] *(to make someone unable to hear anything or unable to hear very well.)*

His mother is going deaf.

The disease will make her go blind.

Go red [Phrase] *(to become red in the face because you are embarrassed or ashamed.)*

Whenever I talked about my brother's past life, he would go red.

He went red as a beetroot.

Tom was very embarrassed and his face went red.

Go dark [Phrase] *(to become suddenly dark.)*

Suddenly the room went dark, and I couldn't see anything.

The sky went very dark suddenly and it started to rain heavily.

Generally accepted [Adverb + Verb] *(accepted by a majority of people.)*

Jack is generally accepted as the top student in the class.

Nowadays, English is generally accepted as the international language.

Get (someone) ready *[Phrase] (to prepare yourself or someone else to do something.)*

It's time to get the kids ready to go to bed.

He's getting ready to go out.

Get (something) ready *[Phrase] (to prepare something.)*

I got the salad ready while my sister cooked the spaghetti.

We should get everything ready before the concert starts.

Get a call *[Verb + Noun] (to receive a phone call from someone.)*

He got a call from his girlfriend at midnight.

My wife keeps getting lots of calls. I wish she would turn off her phone for a while.

Get a shock *[Verb + Noun] (to be very surprised by something bad that happens unexpectedly.)*

She got a shock when she knew her house was robbed.

My sister got a shock when she saw her electricity bill.

Get a ticket *[Verb + Noun] (to get a fine for breaking a traffic law, such as parking illegally, speeding, etc.)*

My cousin got a ticket for speeding last night.

Tom got a ticket for parking his car improperly.

Get angry *[Verb + Adjective] (to become angry about something that you dislike very much.)*

Tom got extremely angry with himself for making such a stupid mistake.

When my dad is in a bad mood, he gets angry easily.

Get back together *[Verb + Adverb] (to become a couple or to start having a relationship with each other again after being apart.)*

Susan just got back together with her ex-boyfriend.

I hope that henry and his wife will get back together.

Get better *[Verb + Adjective] (to improve in skill or ability, to recover from illness.)*

He is getting better at speaking and writing.

Her daughter is still in hospital, but she is gradually getting better.

Get changed *[Verb + Verb] (to take off the clothes you are wearing and put on different ones.)*

She got changed and went to the party.

Your clothes are wet, so you should go and get changed right now.

Get dark *[Verb + Adjective] (to become dark at the end of a day.)*

It was starting to get dark since we left.

What time does it get dark in your country?

Get dressed *[Verb + Adjective] (to put on clothes.)*

He jumped out of bed and quickly got dressed.

My ex-girlfriend nearly always takes ages to get dressed.

Get into trouble *[Verb + Noun] (to become involved in an unpleasant, difficult, or dangerous situation.)*

The plane got into serious trouble soon after taking off.

The company gets into trouble simply because of poor management.

Get lost *[Verb + Adjective] (to become lost, or be misplaced.)*

My little brother got lost in the forest, but luckily dad found him.

The parcel should've arrived last month, so I guess it got lost in the mail.

Get married *[Verb + Adjective] (to officially marry someone; to formally join in* *marriage with another person.)*

Bill and carol are getting married next year.

My parents got married in 1985.

Get old = grow old *[Verb + Adjective] (to become an elderly person.)*

Although my father gets old, he is still able to play golf.

I think I'll have lots of leisure time when I get old.

Get rid of *[Verb + Adjective] (to throw away, give away or remove something that you do not want any longer; to take action so as to be free of (something or someone unpleasant or undesirable))*

I'll never wear this old t-shirt, so I should get rid of it.

I don't like these old clothes anymore, so I'll get rid of all of them.

I can't stand the smoke smell. Do you know how to get rid of it?

Get tired *[Verb + Adjective] (to become tired and feel like resting or sleeping.)*

After running for two kilometers, he suddenly got very tired.

You can suddenly get very tired after playing that game.

Get tired of *[Verb + Adjective] (to become bored or annoyed with something or someone.)*

Tom is getting tired of working for that company. He's going to quit his job.

She gets tired of waiting for her boyfriend to call.

Get to sleep *[Verb + Noun] (to start sleeping.)*

My mother has problems getting to sleep.

Anytime I drink coffee late at night, I always have trouble getting to sleep.

Get upset *[Verb + Adjective] (to become very sad, worried, disappointed, annoyed or* *angry about something.)*

He got very upset to hear that the meeting had been canceled.

Jane gets upset when anyone mentions about her divorce.

Get used to *[Verb + Adjective] (to become accustomed to or familiar with something or someone.)*

Eventually, you'll get used to the traffic of the city.

You'll soon get used to using this electronic device.

Give a hand *[Verb + Noun] (to give someone help, support or assistance.)*

Hey bill, could you give me a hand with these suitcases? They are heavy.

If I have any trouble with my homework, please give me a hand.

Give advice *[Verb + Noun] (to give your opinion or suggestion to somebody about the best thing to do in a particular situation.)*

Peter gave me some expert advice about investing in real estate.

I'm not sure what to do, please give me some advice.

Give birth *[Verb + Noun] (if a mother gives birth, she produces a baby from her body.)*

My sister gave birth to twins.

She gave birth to a daughter.

Give evidence *[Verb + Noun] (to talk and answer questions about what you witnessed or know in a court of law when they answer questions.)*

He was asked to give evidence at the trial.

Jessica agreed to give evidence at the trial.

Give notice *[Verb + Noun] (to formally tell your employer that you will stop working.)*

I've heard that john gave his notice yesterday.

Joe gave her notice yesterday. She is getting a job offer from another company today.

Give permission *[Verb + Noun]* *(to allow or let someone to do something.)*

The English teacher gave tom permission to go home early.

John's parents gave him permission to go to the party.

Give rise to something *[Verb + Noun]* *(to cause or result in something, especially something unpleasant or unexpected.)*

The decisions could give rise to arguments.

Smoking cigarettes and drinking a lot of alcohol can give rise to a range of health problems.

Give someone a call = give someone a ring *[Verb + Noun]* *(to telephone someone; to call (someone) on the telephone.)*

I'll give you a call when I get back from my trip.

If you need to ask me for advice, just give me a call.

Give somebody a chance *[Verb + Noun]* *(to give someone the opportunity to do something.)*

Kids were given the chance to watch cartoons.

Carol was given the chance to show off her singing voice.

Give someone a lift *[Verb + Noun]* *(to give someone a ride (to take somebody somewhere in a car or other vehicle); to make someone feel good, better or happier.)*

I've got to go to the post office. Can you give me a lift?

My car is being repaired. Can you give me a lift to my office on your way to work tomorrow?

Give something a go *[Verb + Noun]* *(to try or attempt to do something, esp. something you've never tried to do before.)*

You should give cooking a go. I'm sure you'll be fine!

Tom was not brave enough to give skydiving a go.

Give thought (to) [Verb + Noun] *(to consider or think about something.)*

After I give some thought to the matter, I will give you a ring.

I hope you'll give what I said some thought and get back to me.

Give up hope [Verb + Noun] *(to stop hoping that something will happen since you believe it's no longer possible.)*

His family still haven't given up hope of finding his brother alive.

Although the doctor said she wouldn't be able to recover, her family never gave up hope.

Give way [Verb + Noun] *(to break or collapse due to weight or pressure from strong forces; to allow other vehicles to go first when moving on the road.)*

The old wooden bridge is threatened to give way, so we need to replace it early.

Drivers must give way to the ambulance.

Go bankrupt [Verb + Adjective] *(to be unable to pay one's debts.)*

The company went bankrupt after only a year in business since their products didn't sell very well.

The company that my uncle had invested in went bankrupt.

Go crazy [Verb + Adjective] *(to become mentally ill (to go insane or go mad); to become very angry about something; to become very excited.)*

She went crazy and said that someone was trying to kill her.

His parents will go crazy if they find out he lied to them.

The crowd went crazy when Cristiano Ronaldo scored a goal.

Go on a date [Verb + Noun] *(to go out with someone romantically.)*

Bill phoned me last night, and we're going on a date next Sunday night.

He called me and we're going on a date next Saturday night.

Peter is very excited to go on a date with Jane.

Go smoothly *[Verb + Adverb]* *(happen or take place without difficulty, problems, or delays.)*

If you want your class presentation to go smoothly, proper preparations must be made.

I hope that tonight's show will go smoothly.

Go unchallenged *[Verb + Adjective]* *(to be accepted without asking questions or criticizing.)*

We couldn't let his comments to go unchallenged.

They couldn't allow bill's claim to go unchallenged.

Go unnoticed *[Verb + Adjective]* *(to not be seen, observed or noticed by someone.)*

I hope peter's hard work doesn't go unnoticed.

His contribution to protecting wild animals hasn't gone unnoticed.

Go wrong *[Verb + Adverb]* *(to not go well, or to happen in a way that causes bad results.)*

Everything is going wrong for me today.

They lost the game. We don't know what went wrong.

Good cause *[Adjective + Noun]* *(an organization, activity or charity that is not managed for profit that helps people in need.)*

His donation will go to a good cause which helps disabled children.

John spent a half of his income on good causes.

Good deal *[Adjective + Noun]* *(a fair deal or fair price.)*

Peter got a good deal on the car.

I think my father will only sell them the house if they give him a good deal.

Good enough *[Adjective + Adverb]* *(be adequately good.)*

This apartment is good enough for me. I won't need to buy a luxury flat.

The hotel is good enough for us. We won't need to find any another one.

Good luck *[Adjective + Noun] (a phrase used to wish someone success or wish fortune on someone.)*

Good luck in your final exam!

Good luck slicing the cucumber thinly. I hope the knife doesn't cut your fingers.

Good time *[Adjective + Noun] (a fun or enjoyable experience; the right moment to do something.)*

We had a good time at the party.

Is this a good time for us to come over?

Great deal of *[Adjective + Noun] (a very large amount of or quantity of something.)*

We spent a great deal of time on this project.

Tom's father gave him a great deal of money.

Greatly appreciate *[Adverb + Verb] (to be grateful for something very much; to admire and value something or someone very much.)*

We greatly appreciated his advice and support.

Your honesty is greatly appreciated.

Growing number (of) *[Adjective + Noun] (an increasing number (of); more and more.)*

A growing number of people are studying English.

We've seen a growing number of people are choosing to study online.

Guilty conscience *[Adjective + Noun]* *(a feeling of shame or remorse experienced by someone after doing something wrong or bad.)*

He has a guilty conscience about the way he treated his classmate.

We could see that she had a guilty conscience about this.

Guilty party *[Adjective + Noun]* *(the person or people who have done something wrong or bad.)*

The guilty party has not been able to identify.

The man was arrested is the guilty party.

Gain access *[Verb + Noun]* *(to get the right to have or use something/ to get the right to enter or reach a place.)*

We haven't been able to gain access to the internet recently.

The police are trying to gain access to the area.

Get soaked to the skin *[Phrase]* *(to be extremely wet/ to wet through someone's clothing to the skin.)*

We were caught in the rain and got soaked to the skin last night.

It started to rain heavily and I got soaked to the skin.

Golden sands *[Adjective + Noun]* *(sands are bright yellow in colour.)*

We wandered for miles along the golden sands.

There are several beaches which are covered with soft golden sands in my country.

Get away from it all *[Phrase]* *(to go somewhere relaxing or peaceful to escape from your usual daily routine.)*

We've decided to go on vacation to get away from it all.

The city is so noisy and crowded, so sometimes I just want to go to the countryside to get away from it all for a few days.

Guided tour *[Adjective + Noun] (if somebody takes you on a guided tour, they will show you around a place of interest and tell you all about what you are seeing or explain facts about the place.)*

We went on a guided tour of the ancient town on the first day of our trip.

Those who first visit the castle will be recommended to go on a guided tour.

Go sightseeing *[Verb + Noun] (to look around the places of interest.)*

We had no time to go sightseeing in Seattle.

I'm planning to go sightseeing in Bali next week.

Get on well with = get along well with *[Phrase] (to have a good relationship with somebody.)*

John gets on very well with his roommates.

Joe and her mother-in-law don't get along well with each other.

Get to know *[Verb + Verb] (to become familiar with someone or something.)*

Sally has just got a new job. I think that she will get to know her new boss and colleagues much better over the next few weeks.

Bill is a bit shy, but you'll find him interesting when you get to know him.

Get into shape *[Verb + Noun] (to become strong, fit and healthy/ to be in good physical condition.)*

If you don't exercise regularly, you won't get into shape.

John wants to get into shape, so he's started working out every day.

Go jogging *[Verb + Noun] (to run at a slow steady speed as a form of exercise.)*

I and my roommates go jogging through the park every morning.

He used to go jogging right after work.

Peter would prefer to play tennis rather than (to go) jogging.

Grab a bite to eat *[Verb + Noun]* *(to get something to eat quickly, especially when you are in a hurry.)*

If you are hungry, let's grab a bite to eat.

The movie will start in 30 minutes, so let's just grab a quick bite to eat.

Give feedback *[Verb + Noun]* *(to offer information or statements of opinion about how well or how badly someone is doing something.)*

His teacher gave him feedback on the test.

I would be grateful if you could give me feedback on my writing.

Graduation ceremony *[Verb + Noun]* *(a ceremony at which you receive an academic degree after finishing your studies at a college or university.)*

Her graduation ceremony will take place on May 22nd.

Tomorrow will be the graduation ceremony of my brother.

Good team player *[Adjective + Noun]* *(a person who works well with other people as part of a team or group.)*

Peter is a good team player. I always like to work with him.

Are you a good team player?

I like football since it teaches me about being a good team player.

Get over the worst *[Verb + Noun]* *(to get through the worst stage of an illness.)*

Joe has got over the worst of her flu.

It took him six months to get over the worst of his illness.

Go private *[Verb + Noun]* *(to choose to pay for medical treatment that is offered by commercial healthcare rather than use the free treatment services offered by the state.)*

I didn't want to wait, so I decided to go private.

If you could afford it, you should go private.

Get a good review *[Verb + Noun] (to receive a positive comment or feedback.)*

His book has got a lot of good reviews from readers so far.

She knew she wasn't going to get a good review from him.

Get a bad review *[Verb + Noun] (to receive a negative comment or feedback.)*

Don't worry if you get a bad review from time to time. Everyone knows that you are not a bad writer.

He felt sad when he got a bad review from a secret shopper.

Go on general release *[Verb + Noun] (if a film goes on general release, it is available to be widely seen in theaters or cinemas.)*

The latest Hollywood film goes on general release this week.

The new film goes on general release later this month.

Get dressed up *[Verb + Adjective] (to put on smart clothes for a special occasion.)*

She always gets dressed up for parties and weddings.

My wife gets dressed up every Saturday.

Go out of fashion *[Verb + Noun] (to become unfashionable.)*

That kind of vehicle went out of fashion many years ago.

Do you think blue jeans will go out of fashion?

Good company *[Adjective + Noun] (someone who people enjoy spending time with.)*

Bill and jack are good company, so I always invite them to my parties.

Joe is such good company. Whenever she comes over my house for dinner, we have a great time.

Go bust *[Phrase] (if a company goes bust, it goes bankrupt since it loses so much money.)*

The company went bust after 2 years in business.

More than 15 companies in the town went bust during the last five months.

Their company went bust after oil prices increased since they couldn't compete with American companies any longer.

Go into business with [Phrase] *(to start working in business with someone.)*

Peter asked me if I agreed to go into business with him.

It wasn't a mistake to go into business with him. We made a lot of money.

You need to create a written agreement if you want to go into business with a partner.

Go it alone [Phrase] *(to do something by yourself without any help or assistance from other people/ (in business) to start your own business.)*

He is going to quit his job as an office worker and go it alone in business.

If they're not willing to help me, I guess I will go it alone.

Get around [Phrase] *(to travel to different places.)*

Without a car, I find it difficult to get around town.

He used a car to get around the city.

Go on tour [Phrase] *(to travel around the country or the world for pleasure.)*

We'd go on the tour.

The rock and roll band will go on tour when their new album is released.

Get caught in the rain [Phrase] *(to be outside when it starts raining suddenly.)*

Did you get caught in the rain?

We were lucky that we didn't get caught in the rain.

You might catch a cold if you get caught in the rain.

Get drenched *[Verb + Adjective] (to get completely wet.)*

He took shelter under a tree to avoid getting drenched in the rain.

She got drenched on the way to work since she didn't have a raincoat.

Get into debt *[Verb + Noun] (if you get into debt, you owe money to someone.)*

Using credit cards could make people get into debt.

Many young people get into debt due to buying unnecessary things that they don't need.

Get back to nature *[Verb + Noun] (if you want to get back to nature, you want to start living in a simple way, often in the country.)*

She decided to escape from the city life and get back to nature.

He wants to get back to nature, enjoys the fresh air and hears some bird songs.

Go viral *[Verb + Adjective] (to rapidly become very popular or well known on the internet through social networking sites, e-mail, etc.)*

Within several days, his blog went viral.

Within 36 hours, her film clip went viral on Facebook and YouTube.

Go trekking *[Verb + Noun] (to go on a long journey on foot, usually for pleasure.)*

We are planning to go trekking in the Himalayas.

Peter and Mary are going trekking in New Zealand.

Go backpacking *[Verb + Noun] (if you go backpacking, you go travelling or go camping with a backpack.)*

Many people like to go backpacking in the mountain.

We're planning to go backpacking in Spain this summer.

Go part-time *[Verb + Adjective] (to do part-time work.)*

He has decided to go part time in the shop.

After returning from maternity leave, she decided to go part-time so that she could spend more time with her son.

Go freelance *[Verb + Adjective]* *(if you freelance, you work as a freelancer.)*

Tom decided to go freelance as a graphic and web designer.

My sister has a baby, so she has decided to go freelance as a writer and editor.

Go on strike = stage a strike *[Phrase]* *(to stop working as a protest because of an argument with an employer about pay levels, working conditions, or job losses.)*

The workers threaten to go on strike because they think their salaries are too low.

The employees went on strike for better wages at noon yesterday.

Get the sack *[Verb + Noun]* *(to be dismissed/ to get fired.)*

He got the sack for always being late.

She got the sack when her boss found out that she had lied about her qualifications.

Go skiing *[Verb + Noun]* *(to slide over snow on skis.)*

We like to go skiing on the mountain.

When is the best time to go skiing in your country?

Go cycling *[Verb + Noun]* *(to ride a bicycle.)*

Tom is planning to go cycling with Mary tomorrow.

I like to go cycling in my free time.

Go fishing *[Verb + Noun]* *(to try to catch fish by using a fishing rod.)*

We like to go fishing on weekends.

He used to go fishing quite often, but now he rarely goes.

I used to go fishing with my father when I was a child.

Go surfing *[Verb + Noun] (to ride on waves in the sea on a surf board.)*

We sometimes go surfing on weekends.

Tom and his friends go surfing every Sunday.

Go climbing *[Verb + Noun] (to climb up mountains for enjoyment and exercise.)*

We go climbing in Scotland every summer.

They are planning to go climbing this weekend.

Go swimming *[Verb + Noun] (to swim for enjoyment and exercise.)*

I and my son go swimming every morning.

Would you like to go swimming in the sea with us?

Go skateboarding *[Verb + Noun] (to stand on a board with four wheels on the bottom and ride.)*

We went skateboarding last Saturday.

Tom goes skateboarding with his friends every Sunday.

Go jogging *[Verb + Noun] (to run at a slow steady speed for exercise.)*

I used to go jogging almost every day.

He likes to go jogging after work.

Go snowboarding *[Verb + Noun] (to ride a snowboard.)*

Tom and his friends go snowboarding every Saturday.

We go snowboarding from time to time in the winter.

Go online *[Verb + Adverb] (to be connected to the internet.)*

Tom usually use his cell phone to go online.

Her busy school schedule doesn't allow her to go online regularly.

Get a degree/diploma = obtain a diploma *[Verb + Noun]* *(to be awarded a qualification after completing a university or college course.)*

Her brother wants to get a degree in engineering.

Jessica decided to obtain a degree in medicine when he was in university.

Go on trial *[Phrase]* *(if someone goes on trial, he/she is being tried in a court of law.)*

She will go on trial for fraud.

He will go on trial next week accused of murdering his wife.

Get to the point = come to the point *[Phrase]* *(to stop talking about unimportant details and start talking about the thing that is most important.)*

I wish she would get/come to the point as quickly as possible.

It took a couple of paragraphs for him to get/come to the point of his argument essay.

Get into conversation (with someone) *[Verb + Noun]* *(to start talking to somebody you've never met before.)*

Tom sat opposite a beautiful girl and they got into conversation.

I met peter at the airport and we got into conversation.

Go on foot *[Phrase]* *(to travel by walking.)*

I go on foot to the school every day.

Peter and tom drove home, but I went on foot.

Go for a walk = go on a walk = take a walk *[Phrase]* *(to walk at a moderate rate for pleasure.)*

Let's go for a walk in the park tomorrow.

I prefer taking a walk rather than going shopping.

Would you like to go on a walk with me tonight?

Go jogging [Phrase] *(to run at a slow steady speed for exercise.)*

I used to go jogging almost every day.

He likes to go jogging after work.

Go running [Phrase] *(to run at a fast speed as a form of exercise.)*

We go running around the park every morning.

How often do you go running?

Go for a run [Phrase] *(to run for pleasure.)*

He goes for a run every day at 6 am.

I usually go for a run after work.

Get started [Phrase] *(to begin doing or working on something.)*

Are you ready to get started?

They couldn't wait to get started on the next project.

You'd better get started on your essay if you want to finish it on time.

Give the chance [Verb + Noun] *(to give someone the opportunity to do something.)*

She gave him the chance to talk to her again.

Mary gave tom the chance to prove to her that he loved her.

COLLOCATIONS/H

Historic city *[Adjective + Noun] (a city that is old and interesting or impressive.)*

London is the historic city of England.

Boston is a historic city with a lot of wonderful restaurants and fine museums.

Have a stopover *[Verb + Noun] (to have a stop during a journey, especially during a flight.)*

We had a stopover in Bangkok.

He had a stopover for three nights in Seattle with his wife and youngest son on their way to Hawaii.

Have a barbecue *[Verb + Noun] (to have a meal at which meat and other food is cooked and eaten outdoors.)*

Let's have a barbecue!

We had a barbecue for the whole family on the beach.

We haven't had a barbecue for a long time, so we plan to have a barbecue party next Saturday.

Have a thirst for knowledge *[Verb + Noun] (to desire to know or learn more about something.)*

He has a thirst for knowledge and learns quickly.

She is a quick learner and has a thirst for knowledge.

Hand in your resignation *[Verb + Noun] (to submit your resignation.)*

Tom is thinking of handing in his resignation.

Alice has finally decided to hand in her resignation at the bank.

Have no option (but to do something) *[Verb + Noun] (to have no other* *choice (except to do something))*

I had no option but to call the police.

Tom had no option but to admit the truth.

After his appalling behavior, his boss had no option but to fire him.

Hectic lifestyle *[Adjective + Noun] (a busy lifestyle.)*

He tries to get away from his hectic lifestyle.

Almost young people these days lives a hectic lifestyle.

High-yield investment *[Adjective + Noun] (investments with high rates of return.)*

This is a high-yield investment opportunity.

A large amount of money was invested in high-yield investment programs in Canada.

Handwritten manuscript *[Adjective + Noun] (a manuscript that is written by using a pen or a pencil, instead of being typed.)*

Not a lot of people today would like to read a handwritten manuscript.

He is going to submit his handwritten manuscript to a publisher tomorrow.

High street *[Adjective + Noun] (the main street of a town where there are many shops, banks, and other businesses.)*

Our fashion shop is located in the high street opposite the Italian restaurant.

Many people go shopping at retail outlets on the high street.

Home game *[Noun + Noun] (a game played in a team's own geographic area, such as a stadium, park, home ground, etc.)*

He played the last home game of his football career yesterday.

We can't wait to see our favorite team's next home game.

Heated debate *[Adjective + Noun] (an argument or a discussion in which people express different opinions in an angry and excited way.)*

Hot topics often cause some heated debate.

There has been heated debate about whether mobile phones should be allowed in school.

The murder case became the subject of heated debate within the legal profession.

Higher education *[Adjective + Noun] (education and training at a college or university where subjects are studied at an advanced level.)*

Higher education is given in colleges and universities.

He inspires all his students to pursue higher education.

Have breakfast/ lunch/ dinner *[Verb + Noun] (to eat breakfast/ lunch/ dinner.)*

We usually have breakfast/ lunch/ dinner at that restaurant.

Would you like to have breakfast/ lunch/ dinner with me?

Highly likely *[Adverb + Adjective] (very likely)* # ***highly unlikely*** *[Adverb + Adjective] (very unlikely)*

It's highly likely that the thieves don't know how much this property is worth.

It's highly likely that it will rain tomorrow.

It is highly unlikely that tom will be late.

Highly unusual *[Adverb + Adjective] (very unusual; really different from what is usual or normal.)*

He has a highly unusual name.

It's highly unusual to have a goalkeeper as the captain of a football team.

It is highly unusual for her to be able to get pregnant so easily while having endometriosis.

Highly successful = very successful = extremely successful *[Adverb + Adjective] (having achieved a lot.)*

He has a highly successful career

Mark is highly successful in the real estate business

Highly competitive *[Adverb + Adjective] (very competitive.)*

The automobile market in Japan is highly competitive.

Graduating students have to fight for jobs in a highly competitive market.

Highly profitable *[Adverb + Adjective] (very likely to make money; very likely to result in a profit or an advantage.)*

They have a highly profitable line of products.

It has developed into a highly profitable business over the years.

Highly effective *[Adverb + Adjective] (producing a very successful result.)*

Aspirin is a highly effective treatment for her headache.

Reading books is a highly effective way to learn new things.

Highly controversial *[Adverb + Adjective] (causing a lot of angry public discussion and disagreement.)*

Death penalty is a highly controversial subject.

The issue of the abortion is highly controversial.

Highly educated *[Adverb + Verb] (having a good level of education/ knowledge; having a high standard of education.)*

He is probably the most highly educated person in the town.

Lawyers should be highly educated.

Have a baby *[Verb + Noun] (to give birth to a very young child)*

My sister had a baby boy last year.

Lucy is going to have a baby next month.

Have a word [Verb + Noun] (to talk about something with somebody)

I would like to have a word with you for a few minutes.

Could I have a word with you for a few minutes?

Have access (to) [Verb + Noun] (to be able to use or benefit from something)

No one is allowed to have access to his computer while he's away.

Students should be given chances to have access to good book resources.

Have an effect (on) = have an impact (on) [Verb + Noun] (to cause a change)

Stress can have negative effects on the immune system.

The radiation leak has had an adverse impact on the environment.

Have room [Verb + Noun] (to have enough space for something or someone)

We don't have room for a sports car in our house.

We have room for you in the car.

Have sex = make love [Verb + Noun] (to have sexual contact with someone)

That was the first time they have sex.

Not all people want to have a baby when they have sex.

Jack was shocked to learn that his wife had had sex before she was married.

Have the chance (to) = have an opportunity (to) = get a chance (to) [Verb + Noun] (to have the opportunity to do something, especially something that you want to do)

I usually pay my brother a visit whenever I have the chance.

If he had the chance to study abroad, he would go to the US.

Have time *[Verb + Noun] (to have enough time to do something)*

I'm sorry. I have tons of work to do today. I don't have time to go to the cinema with you. See you another time.

I usually visit my parents when I have time.

Have trouble *[Verb + Noun] (to find it difficult to do something)*

We are having trouble with this new software.

She often has trouble finding good carers for her children.

Have an accident *[Verb + Noun] (to urinate or excrete without intending to do it.)*

Her four-year-old son has an accident at night sometimes.

Tom's mom asked him to go to the toilet before they left in order that he wouldn't have an accident in the car.

Have an argument *[Verb + Noun] (to angrily disagree in a conversation or discussion; to have an angry disagreement between people in a conversation or discussion.)*

He had an argument with his girlfriend yesterday.

They had an argument with the waitress about the bill.

Have a break = take a break *[Verb + Noun] (to have a short period of time to rest, eat, drink, go to toilet, etc. before starting doing something again.)*

We'll have/ take a break at 11.30 a.m.

Jack decided to have/ take a break from college and do some travelling.

Have a conversation *[Verb + Noun] (to have a talk with someone about something.)*

Peter had a long telephone conversation with his girlfriend.

Sometimes it's not much interesting to have a long telephone conversation.

Have difficulty (in) doing something *[Phrase] (to have a problem; to be in a difficult situation.)*

I had difficulty (in) persuading him to leave.

Her brother still has difficulty walking after the accident.

Have a dream *[Verb + Noun] (to experience a series of events or images that happen in your mind when you are sleeping.)*

He had a very strange dream last night.

Julie had a vivid dream about her old house.

Have a nightmare *[Verb + Noun] (to have a very upsetting or frightening dream.)*

He had a nightmare about the accident.

She had a terrifying nightmare last night.

Have an experience *[Verb + Noun] (to have knowledge or skill from doing something.)*

Susan has the experience of working with kids.

I think mark has the experience for the job

Have a feeling *[Verb + Noun] (to be conscious of something but not certain about it.)*

Peter had the feeling someone was following him.

He has a feeling he has met her before.

Have fun *[Verb + Noun] (to have pleasure, enjoyment, or entertainment.)*

We had a lot of fun at her party.

Have fun (= enjoy yourself)!

Have a good time *[Verb + Noun] (to have an enjoyable or fun experience.)*

We had a good time at Lucy's party.

We shared many good times when we were in high school.

Have a party = throw a party [Verb + Noun] *(to organize a social event at which people meet to have fun by eating and drinking, dancing, playing games etc., often in order to celebrate a special occasion.)*

They're having a big party for their 10th wedding anniversary next week.

We are having a small party tomorrow.

Have a problem with sth/sb [Verb + Noun] *(to find something annoying; to not like or approve of something.)*

His parents had a problem with him playing games all day long.

I have a problem with people using their phones in the library.

Have a try = have a go [Verb + Noun] *(to attempt to do something.)*

Why didn't you have a try at convincing her?

I'll have a try to convince him to come.

Happy ending [Adjective + Noun] *(the last part of a story, a novel, film, etc., in which the plot achieves a happy resolution.)*

My son really loves this fairy tale since it has a happy ending.

Many films and novels don't have happy endings.

Happy hour [Adjective + Noun] *(a period of time, usually in late afternoon and early evening, when alcoholic drinks are sold at a lower price than usual in a bar or a pub.)*

Happy hour in our bar runs from 5:00 to 7:30.

Low priced drinks and selling to underaged drinkers.

We'll have to pay full price for our drinks if we miss happy hour; so, we need to halt it.

Hard work [Adjective + Noun] *(any activity that requires a lot of energy, effort or endurance.)*

It takes hard work to be successful in politics.

My parents always taught me the value of hard work.

Hard to believe *[Phrase]* *(not easily believed; difficult to believe.)*

Jane found it hard to believe that tom was a real doctor.

His story was hard to believe.

Hard to see *[Phrase]* *(difficult to see; difficult to do, understand or imagine.)*

Tom found it hard to see the board, so his teacher suggested getting his eyes tested.

It is really hard to see what else I can do now.

It's hard to see how they can lose since they're a much better team.

Hard to tell *[Phrase]* *(difficult to know or deduce something.)*

Hardly any almost none there's hardly any food left, so I'd better go to the market.

Soon after bertha found the box of chocolates, there were hardly any left.

Hardly ever *[Adverb + Adverb]* *(almost never, very seldom.)*

We hardly ever see him at the weekends.

His father hardly ever smiles.

My sister hardly ever stays up late at night.

Hardly likely *[Adverb + Adjective]* *(very unlikely)*

My boss might agree to let me do it, but it's hardly likely.

It is hardly likely that the car can run on solar energy.

Hate to think *[Verb + Verb]* *(do not want to think or imagine about something because it is unpleasant or upsetting.)*

Peter hates to think how much money he has spent on gambling.

Joe hates to think she has lost over $5000.

Have a chat *[Verb + Noun]* *(to have a friendly, informal conversation with someone.)*

Mark nearly always enjoy having a chat with his girlfriend before going to bed.

He gave me a call and we had a long chat.

Have a go *[Verb + Noun]* *(to try or attempt to do something; to criticize someone angrily/strongly.)*

I've never sat on a horse so far, but I'll have a go.

Peter's wife had a go at him over breakfast this morning

Have a look at something = take a look at something *[Verb + Noun]* *(to look at something with attention.)*

Can I have a look at your new car?

She asked the doctor to take a look at her cut.

Have a right *[Verb + Noun]* *(to have a moral or legal entitlement to do something.)*

You have no right to push me aside.

David has the right to vote in the US election.

Have a word (with somebody) *[Verb + Noun]* *(to talk with someone privately about something.)*

I think you should have a word with Jane and see what she thinks.

Peter called and had a word with me last night.

Have got *[Verb + Verb]* *(to have, own, or possess.)*

Peter has got a new job.

I have got 2 children.

Have got to = have to *[Verb + Verb] (must)*

Jane's doctor said she has got to take the pills.

You have got to pay a fine.

Healthy diet *[Adjective + Noun] (balanced diet; a diet that contains sufficient amounts of necessary nutrients required for body's health.)*

If you have a healthy diet, you will get all the vitamins you need.

A healthy diet is what we need to live healthily.

Heavily armed *[Adverb + Adjective] (carrying many dangerous weapons.)*

That is a group of heavily armed men.

Most of the terrorists are heavily armed.

Heavy drinker *[Adjective + Noun] (a person who drinks a lot of alcohol.)*

I don't drink much alcohol, whereas my brother is a heavy drinker.

Luckily, my father is not a heavy drinker.

Heavy losses *[Adjective + Noun] (when a lot of people die.)*

The accident caused heavy losses.

The floods caused heavy losses.

Heavy schedule *[Adjective + Noun] (a schedule which is full of activity, or very busy.)*

I've got a heavy schedule this afternoon, but I can come over your house for dinner tonight.

My schedule is very heavy today, so I won't have time to play tennis.

Heavy smoker *[Adjective + Noun] (a person who smokes a lot of cigarettes.)*

My brother is a heavy smoker. He smokes at least 30 cigarettes a day.

Jane really hates heavy smokers.

Heavy traffic *[Adjective + Noun] (the traffic that has so many vehicles or people that it is difficult to move around.)*

Heavy traffic took place on the roads this morning.

Carol always blames the heavy traffic when she is late for work.

High quality *[Adjective + Noun] (very good quality)*

This range of wines is all high quality.

The quality of the food in this restaurant is higher than others.

High standard *[Adjective + Noun] (very good standard)*

Mark always produces work of a high standard.

The standards of health-care service in this private hospital are incredibly high.

Highly regarded = well regarded *[Adverb + Verb] (be respected and admired by many people.)*

The airline is highly regarded by passengers.

My father is very highly regarded as a doctor.

Highly unlikely *[Adverb + Adjective] (very unlikely to be true or to occur.)*

It's highly unlikely that Susan will invite her ex-boyfriend to the wedding.

The traffic is very heavy, so it's highly unlikely that she'll arrive on time.

Hold an election *[Verb + Noun] (to conduct an election (an occasion when people vote for someone to represent them).*

As far as people concern, it is necessary to hold an election every four years.

The election will be held on September the 26th.

Hold an inquiry *[Verb + Noun]* *(to conduct an official inquiry (the process of asking questions).*

Police are holding an inquiry into his business affairs.

The official inquiry into the incident is now being held.

Hold hands *[Verb + Noun]* *(if two people hold hands, each person holds another person's nearest hand, typically as a sign of affection.)*

He was holding hands with Mary.

When you cross the street, please hold henry's hand.

Hold someone hostage *[Verb + Noun]* *(to capture or keep someone as a hostage and demand something in exchange for their release.)*

He was held hostage for 14 hours before being released.

The terrorists are still holding 12 people in the airplane.

Hold/keep/take sb prisoner *[Verb + Noun]* *(to catch and force somebody to stay somewhere so that they cannot escape.)*

Of 9,000 soldiers, 5,000 were killed, wounded, or held prisoner.

The gunmen have held the pilot and several passengers for 25 hours.

Hold talks *[Verb + Noun]* *(to have discussions between important people from opposing sides about an issue or a situation.)*

Informal talks will be held between the management and union officials.

Trade talks will be held in Washington this month.

Honest mistake *[Adjective + Noun]* *(something that anyone could be wrong about; a mistake that wasn't made intentionally.)*

I gave him the wrong phone number, but it was an honest mistake.

It was just an honest mistake, so don't worry about it.

Hope so *[Verb + Adverb]* *(used to express that you hope something to happen or be* *true.)*

"Will you be able to come to dinner Saturday?" "I hope so".

I'm not sure whether I will pass the driving test, but I hope so.

Human error *[Adjective + Noun] (a mistake caused by a person, as contrasted with a mechanical or electronic malfunction.)*

The train crash was blamed on human error.

Investigators concluded that the accident was caused by human error.

Hurt sb's feelings *[Verb + Noun] (to upset someone or to make someone feel bad by being insensitive to their feelings.)*

It hurts my feelings when you talk that way.

I don't want to hurt my girlfriend's feelings, so I will not say that she has a terrible singing voice.

Heavy snow *[Adjective + Noun] (a large amount of snow.)*

A heavy snow was falling during the night.

The train was delayed for several hours by a heavy snow.

Heavy clouds *[Adjective + Noun] (thick clouds/ dense cloud.)*

There are heavy clouds in the sky.

Look! Heavy clouds are spreading across the sky.

Holiday brochure *[Noun + Noun] (a thin book or magazine containing pictures and details of holiday packages.)*

We've decided to go on holiday at a resort in Hawaii after looking through a holiday brochure.

I've lost my holiday brochure. May I use yours?

Holiday destination *[Noun + Noun] (a popular place where someone or something is going for a holiday.)*

The Greek island is a popular holiday destination for those who enjoy the sun and the sea.

Tunisia is supposed to be an ideal holiday destination for those who like the sun.

Holiday of a lifetime [Noun + Noun] *(a very special holiday or the best holiday that you will ever have (you will only take once))*

Our trip to Hawaii was the holiday of a lifetime.

I took my whole family on a holiday of a lifetime to Victoria Falls.

Holiday resort [Noun + Noun] *(a place usually with a lot of hotels, bars, and restaurants where lots of people go on holiday/vacation.)*

Blackpool is a popular holiday resort in England.

Rimini is widely known as a thriving holiday resort in Italy.

Hordes of tourists [Noun + Noun] *(large and excited crowds of tourists.)*

Hordes of tourists arrive in Las Vegas every summer.

There are always hordes of tourists flocking to Hawaii in the summer.

Have something in common [Verb + Noun] *(to share similar interests, experiences, beliefs, attitudes, opinions, or other characteristics with someone else.)*

My girlfriend is very nice, and we have a lot in common.

Peter and Rosie don't have anything in common. I don't understand why they've decided to get married to each other.

Have ups and downs [Phrase] *(if someone has ups and downs, they experience a mixture of good times and bad times.)*

I have encountered with ups and downs in my life.

The relationship between peter and Joe has had a lot of ups and downs.

Hit it off [Phrase] *(to be friendly and become good friends with each other quickly.)*

When I started a conversation with Helen in the bar, we hit it off, and had a great time together.

I really hit it off with Rosie and employed her immediately without needing an interview.

Have a sweet tooth [Verb + Noun] *(if you have a sweet tooth, you enjoy sweet foods, especially candy, pastries and chocolate.)*

Tom definitely has a sweet tooth, he loves all kinds of sweet foods.

My son has a sweet tooth. He eats chocolate all the time.

Home-cooked food [Adjective + Noun] *(food which is prepared and eaten at home.)*

I enjoy all kinds of wholesome home - cooked food which are made by my mom.

My father prefers home-cooked food rather than street food.

Higher education [Adjective + Noun] *(education provided by a college or university that is followed after high school.)*

Her parents encourage her to pursue higher education.

Many women have decided to pursue higher education and careers instead of getting married and giving birth to children.

High-powered job [Adjective + Noun] *(a job which is very important and powerful in a company or organization, usually involves a great deal of responsibility.)*

My father has a high-powered job as an attorney.

His high-powered job as a director at a large company gave him a complete nervous breakdown.

Holiday entitlement [Noun + Noun] *(the number of days of paid holiday during a year that an employee or a worker is allowed to take.)*

There were 5 days of holiday entitlement john did not use during his sickness absence.

The employees were grateful to their employer when they received more than the minimum holiday entitlement.

Heavy cold *[Adjective + Noun] (a bad cold.)*

He caught a heavy cold, so he couldn't attend the class.

She was suffered from a heavy cold last week.

Hall of residence *[Noun + Noun] (a college or university dormitory where students live.)*

I stayed in a hall of residence when I was in the first year at university.

Most students who study at the college stay in a hall of residence.

Home comforts *[Noun + Noun] (things that make your home more comfortable or pleasant.)*

My mom misses her home comforts when she is away.

I always like my home comforts.

House-warming party *[Noun + Noun] (a party to celebrate someone's move into a new home.)*

We are planning to have a house-warming party next week.

They threw a huge house-warming party last night.

Have an eye for something *[Phrase] (to be able to understand, recognize, and judge something wisely, especially something attractive, valuable, of good quality etc.)*

My father has an eye for antiques.

She has a sharp eye for jewels.

He has a good eye for paintings.

Hide one's light under a bushel *[Phrase] (to keep quiet or conceal one's talents, ideas or accomplishments.)*

I didn't realize that bill could play the guitar – he's been hiding his light under a bushel.

Please don't hide your light under a bushel. We know you can play this game very well.

High-rise flats *[Adjective + Noun]* *(flats in a very tall building.)*

She's living in a high-rise flat with two balconies.

They don't like living in a high-rise flat since their kids cannot get out to play easily.

Huge following *[Noun + Noun]* *(a person or organization that has a large number of fans.)*

The band has a huge following in Europe.

He has won a huge following of music fans in New Zealand.

Home schooling *[Noun + Noun]* *(the process of educating children at home by their parents rather than in a school.)*

Many parents have chosen home schooling for their children.

As parents, we should consider home schooling for our kids.

Have a whale of time = have a fantastic time *[Phrase]* *(to have an exciting or fun time (enjoy yourself a lot))*

We had a whale of time together in Vancouver.

We did have a fantastic time at Woolley firs.

Heavy workload *[Adjective + Noun]* *(a large amount of work that is expected to be done within a specific amount of time.)*

Students are complaining about their heavy workloads.

John was suffering from stress caused by his heavy workload.

Have a vivid imagination *[Verb + Noun]* *(if someone has a vivid imagination, they are able to imagine ideas, images, etc. very easily.)*

Mary is smart and has a vivid imagination.

My son is creative and has a vivid imagination.

Hurt someone's feelings *[Verb + Noun] (to offend, upset or emotionally hurt someone/ to cause someone emotional pain.)*

I'm sorry - I didn't intend to hurt your feelings by telling you that.

You'll hurt her feelings when you talk that way.

Have an affair *[Verb + Noun] (to have sex or an intimate relationship with someone outside marriage.)*

Her husband is having an affair.

His wife denied that she was having an affair.

Her husband hasn't had an affair since he got married.

Happy couple *[Verb + Noun] (two people in a happy romantic relationship, especially two people who have just got married or will soon get married.)*

The happy couple have decided to get married next month.

After traditional ceremonies, the happy couple were given paper money by their friends and relatives.

Have experience (in something) *[Verb + Noun] (to have knowledge and skill in doing something or in a particular field.)*

He has 10 years of experience in the computer industry.

Carol has a lot of experience in sales and marketing.

Have a brief chat *[Verb + Noun] (to have a friendly, informal conversation with someone which lasts only for a short time.)*

Sarah's manager said he wanted to have a brief chat with her.

Peter enjoys having a brief chat with his girlfriend before going to bed.

Have a quick word *[Verb + Noun] (to speak to someone for a short time.)*

We had a quick word with Jane after her performance.

Could I have a quick word with you about something?

Heated argument *[Adjective + Noun] (an extremely angry disagreement.)*

They were engaged in a very heated argument, and they were shouting at each other.

Peter got into a heated argument with a stranger yesterday.

Jane lost her job after a heated argument with her boss.

Have a burning desire *[Verb + Noun] (if you have a burning desire for something, you have a strong feeling of wanting to have or to do it.)*

He has a burning desire for success.

She has a burning desire for mastery of the Japanese language.

Have a particular liking for *[Phrase] (to have a feeling of enjoying something or someone.)*

My father has a particular liking for classical music.

His mother doesn't have a particular liking for his girlfriend.

Have a clue (about something) *[Verb + Noun] (to know or have knowledge about something about something.)*

A: how did she know her husband was having a relationship with another girl?

B: she had a clue when she found a gift that he gave the girl.

A: do you know what her phone number is?

B: I don't have a clue!

Not have a clue/have no clue = have no idea *[Verb + Noun] (to have no information or no knowledge of or about something.)*

A: "what is the price of his new car?"

B: "I'm sorry, I don't have a clue."

Tom doesn't have a clue about how to fix a dishwasher.

Have a snack [Verb + Noun] (to eat a small amount of food, usually between regular meals.)

We had a snack after lunch.

My mom's made some sandwiches so we could have a snack on the way.

Hit the rocks [Verb + Noun] (to encounter difficulties or troubles in a relationship.)

Their marriage has hit the rocks lately.

They've been best friends for nearly 5 years, but their friendship has hit the rocks recently.

COLLOCATIONS/I

Icy cold *[Adverb + Adjective] (extremely cold.)*

It was an icy-cold night in London.

The water in this ocean is always icy cold.

It's common knowledge that *[Phrase] (something that almost everyone knows; something that is widely known.)*

It's common knowledge that she is in a relationship.

It is common knowledge that several teachers at that university are incompetent.

Impart knowledge to someone *[Verb + Noun] (to transfer knowledge to someone.)*

An educator's job is to impart knowledge to learners.

My responsibility in teaching is to impart knowledge to my students.

Icy wind *[Adjective + Noun] (extremely cold wind.)*

The door was opening and an icy wind swept through the house.

An icy wind was blowing all night.

Ideas flow *[Noun + Verb] (ideas follow each other in a natural way without anything stopping, especially in an easy.)*

His ideas flow smoothly in the essay because of his skillful use of varied sentence structures.

The ideas flow freely from least to most important.

In-flight entertainment *[Adjective + Noun] (films, music, etc. Which are provided during flight in an aircraft to entertain passengers.)*

The in-flight entertainment was excellent, and the seats were comfortable.

The children felt bored because the in-flight entertainment on the plane was not very good.

Ill effects *[Adjective + Noun]* *(problems or damage caused by something.)*

Many people have been suffering ill effects from the contamination of the river.

Henry will suffer no ill effects if he stops taking the drug.

Ill health *[Adjective + Noun]* *(a state of poor health, especially over a long period.)*

My uncle retired at 55 because of ill health.

She was forced to retire because of ill health.

Immediate action *[Adjective + Noun]* *(action taken right away, or without delay.)*

We must take immediate action to solve this problem.

Immediate family *[Adjective + Noun]* *(someone's closest relatives by birth, meaning only their spouse, children, siblings and parents, spouse's siblings and parents.)*

It is usually good to do business with immediate family.

After his death, only members of his immediate family were invited to the funeral.

Impose restrictions *[Verb + Noun]* *(to place limits on particular actions or activities.)*

The government has imposed restrictions on trade with foreign companies.

A range of new restrictions will be imposed on food imports to protect people's health.

Inextricably linked *[Adverb + Verb]* *(if two or more things are inextricably linked, they are so closely connected that you cannot separate them.)*

In tom's mind, the two ideas are inextricably linked.

His work as a lawyer and his experiences in life are inextricably linked.

Innocent victim *[Adjective + Noun] (a person who was guiltless or wasn't involved in the events or actions that harmed them.)*

Jack was a completely innocent victim.

Most innocent victims of drone attacks are the elderly people.

Insect bite *[Noun + Noun] (a sting or bite into skin caused by an insect.)*

Ointment is used to soothe for insect bites

A bluebottle gave tom the most painful insect bite he has ever had.

Inside information *[Adjective + Noun] (important information about a company or organization only known by people inside the company or organization.)*

The bank's accountant was sent to prison for giving inside information the thieves.

He was convicted of supplying inside information to stockbrokers.

Intense pressure *[Adjective + Noun] (very strong or extreme pressure.)*

Davis's been under intense pressure.

Since the video was posted online, the minister has been under intense pressure to resign.

Internal injury *[Adjective + Noun] (any injury to the organs; an injury inside the body.)*

The young man died due to the internal injury.

Most of the internal injuries are caused by road accidents.

Internal organ *[Adjective + Noun] (a main organ inside the body.)*

The heart is one of the internal organs.

His liver is damaged, but his other internal organs are fairly healthy.

Invest heavily *[Verb + Adverb] (to invest a lot of money in something to improve or develop it.)*

John has invested heavily in the bond market.

The US government has invested heavily in education.

Irreparable damage *[Adjective + Noun] (damage that no monetary compensation can cure, it is too serious to repair.)*

Their relationship cannot be repaired, it is the irreparable damage.

Damage to the building was irreparable.

Issue a permit *[Verb + Noun] (to give somebody an official document that gives them permission to do something.)*

The city council had refused to issue a permit for the parade.

I can't remember who issued the parking permit.

Internet security *[Noun + Noun] (a process to take actions to protect against threats or attacks over the internet/ internet safety.)*

Internet security is very important nowadays.

We need to improve internet security to keep hackers out of our important business information.

Intensive course *[Adjective + Noun] (a course that involves lots of teaching or training in a short period of time.)*

He attended an intensive course in business writing 3 months ago.

This is an intensive language course for the beginning students.

Interest payment *[Noun + Noun] (a payment of interest on a loan or mortgage.)*

I bought a bond, and I got an interest payment every six months.

He got an interest payment of $25.

Internet banking *[Verb + Noun] (the system that allows someone to use the internet to put in or take out money from their bank account.)*

I made the payment through internet banking.

He doesn't often go to a bank because he always uses internet banking.

Internet banking is a banking option that allows people to carry out money transfers 24 hours a day.

Incurable disease *[Adjective + Noun] (a disease that cannot be cured.)*

He was diagnosed with an incurable disease.

She is suffering from an incurable disease.

Infectious disease *[Adjective + Noun] (a disease caused by microorganisms, such as bacteria, protozoans, fungi, or viruses.)*

Chickenpox, mumps, and measles are infectious diseases.

He had a nasty infectious disease.

Inner city *[Adjective + Noun] (the central part of a city where a lot of poverty and other social problems exist.)*

They are children from the inner city.

Poor students who are living in the inner city are mostly at a disadvantage.

Immediate family *[Adjective + Noun] (a family unit including parents, brothers and sisters, husband or wife, and children.)*

Only the immediate family is allowed to visit the patient.

His immediate family received more than $50,000 in assistance.

Intense dislike *[Adjective + Noun] (if you have an intense dislike for something or someone, you extremely dislike it/ him/ her.)*

Lucy has an intense dislike for her father's friend.

Peter has an intense dislike for his neighbor's dogs.

Tom has an intense dislike for Thai food because it's too spicy.

COLLOCATIONS/J

Job performance *[Noun + Noun] (activities relates to a job that are executed by an employee.)*

He was fired because of his poor job performance.

We've been extremely satisfied with her job performance.

Job interview *[Noun + Noun] (a meeting in which an employer asks an applicant questions to see whether they would be suitable for a position of employment.)*

He'd been for several job interviews but hadn't been offered a job yet.

Peter did very well on the job interview

Job loss *[Noun + Noun] (a situation in which a person lose his or her jobs.)*

Large debts are caused by job losses.

Funding cuts will cause job losses

Job opportunity *[Noun + Noun] (an opportunity of finding an employment.)*

The government should encourage companies to provide more job opportunities for the unemployed.

This is an area with few job opportunities.

Joint account *[Adjective + Noun] (a bank account in the names of two or more people and subject to withdrawals by each.)*

Many married couples share joint accounts.

All owners of a joint account must be responsible for any liabilities in connection with the account.

Joint effort *[Adjective + Noun] (something that is done by two or more people working together.)*

The math homework was a joint effort between the two of us.

The experiment was a joint effort, with contributions from many students.

Joint owners *[Adjective + Noun]* *(two or more people or organizations who share ownership of something, such as a property, business, etc. together.)*

Henry and his wife are joint owners of their house.

Peter and his friends are joint owners of the company.

Jump to a conclusion *[Verb + Noun]* *(to decide, guess, evaluate or judge something without a sufficient examination of the facts.)*

Don't jump to conclusions! Perhaps it was her father who she was having dinner with.

Let's find out more before jumping to any conclusions. Wait until we hear what he has to say.

Just about *[Adverb + Adverb]* *(almost exactly; very nearly.)*

John can do just about anything when he's on his game because he has a good understanding of it.

I've just about finished my essay.

Just now *[Adverb + Adverb]* *(a very short time ago; at this moment.)*

I saw her just now.

It's just now raining just now, but it is going to stop soon.

Job satisfaction *[Noun + Noun]* *(a feeling of enjoyment that someone derives from their job.)*

When I choose a career, job satisfaction is always the most important factor.

Many workers are more interested in job satisfaction than in earning high salaries.

Levels of job satisfaction have increased over the last few years.

Junk mail *[Noun + Noun]* *(letter or email which consists mostly of advertising* *products or services that's sent to people who haven't asked for it and do not want it.)*

Peter's inbox is full of junk mail.

If you have an email address, you will be likely to receive lots of junk mail or spam.

Junk food *[Noun + Noun] (food that is not healthy, esp. Contains lots of fat, salt, sugar, etc., but it is quick and easy to eat.)*

My kids aren't allowed to eat so much junk food.

She ate so much junk food that she became overweight and ill.

Jump to the conclusion *[Verb + Noun] (to judge or decide something hastily.)*

I should not jump to the conclusion that what she told me is a lie.

You should not jump to the conclusion that he could not afford your house.

COLLOCATIONS/K

Keep a diary *[Verb + Noun] (to write regularly in a diary.)*

Carol kept a diary while she was traveling in japan. This helps her remember all the things she did.

I kept a diary when I was in college, but I do not nowadays.

Keep a promise *[Verb + Noun] (to fulfill your promise; to do what you said that you would do.)*

If you can't keep a promise, you shouldn't make it.

Joe always keeps her promises, so she'll do what she said.

Keep a secret *[Verb + Noun] (to not tell anyone else information that is meant to be a secret.)*

Jane always knows how to keep a secret.

If you promise to keep it a secret, I will tell you what happened.

Keep an appointment *[Verb + Noun] (to go to an appointment that you have arranged on time.)*

Tom couldn't keep the appointment, so he called his doctor and changed it to another time.

Henry failed to keep his appointment.

Keep someone busy *[Verb + Adjective] (to give someone many things to do, often as a way of filling up time.)*

We've got a lot of work to keep us busy for weeks.

Running the company keeps john busy almost every day.

Keep going *[Verb + Verb] (to continue moving forward without stopping; to continue doing something although it is difficult.)*

Jane walked right past me and just kept going.

Turn left at the mall, and then just keep going until seeing the bank.

We forced ourselves to keep going although we felt exhausted.

Cheryl had to keep going for the sake of her children.

Keep quiet *[Verb + Adjective] (to not say anything or to make very little noise.)*

Jack gave his dog a bone to keep him quiet.

We could not keep quiet during the horror film.

Keep records *[Verb + Noun] (to store all the documents, detailed information relating to a company's or organization's activities.)*

The exact numbers will never be known due to poorly keeping records.

All the company records, including net profits, are kept very well.

Keep safe *[Verb + Adjective] (to prevent loss or damage.)*

Please keep your passport safe during your trip in foreign countries.

I must keep the data safe, otherwise, I will be in trouble if I lose it.

Keep sb waiting *[Verb + Verb] (to make someone stay in one place and wait for you.)*

I was kept waiting outside her office for nearly an hour.

Don't keep me waiting for your email reply.

Keep score *[Verb + Noun] (to keep a record of the score in a game or contest.)*

In a professional basketball match, the referee keeps score.

If you are a golfer, you'll have to keep your own scores.

Keep still *[Verb + Adjective] (to not move.)*

Please keep still while I'm taking your photos.

Henry has trouble keeping still in class.

Keep (someone or something) still [Phrase] *(to make someone or something silent or less noisy.)*

Please keep the baby still.

Keep your phone still, please.

Keep your balance [Verb + Noun] *(to remain steady in a position without losing control or falling.)*

Jane grabbed the young man to keep her balance.

If you are drunk, you are unlikely to keep your balance.

Key issue [Adjective + Noun] *(one of the most important issues.)*

High unemployment is the key issue facing the new government.

Public education will be one of the key issues in the election campaign

Key role [Adjective + Noun] *(one of the most important roles.)*

Schools play a key role in society.

The media play a key role in influencing people's opinions.

The kidney plays a key role in the removal of waste products from the blood.

Keynote address [Noun + Noun] *(the main speech or lecture given at a large meeting, conference, or seminar, etc.)*

Mr. Thompson will be delivering the keynote address at this year's conference.

John made some very interesting points in his keynote address.

Keynote speaker [Noun + Noun] *(who gives the keynote address at a formal gathering such as a conference, seminar, meeting, etc.)*

Senator Williams is an inspiring keynote speaker.

The CEO of Apple Corporation was the keynote speaker at the conference.

Kill time *[Verb + Noun]* *(to waste time by doing unimportant things; to do something to help the time pass.)*

When I have to kill time, I usually read a novel on my kindle.

While I am waiting for the bus, I usually check Facebook to kill time.

Know best *[Verb + Adverb]* *(to know or understand better than someone else what the best thing to do is.)*

When it comes to children's toys, your son knows best.

My sister thinks she knows best when it comes to dealing with her own daughter.

Know better *[Verb + Adverb]* *(to be wise, experienced, or well-trained enough to know that it's better not to do something.)*

Don't blame my little daughter. She's just a child and she doesn't know (any) better.

There's no excuse for your behavior. You are old enough to know better.

Children should know better than to accept a lift from a stranger.

Know the score *[Verb + Noun]* *(to know all the important facts in a situation or the truth about something, especially when it is unpleasant.)*

I know the score, so there's no point trying to fool me.

Tom knows the score, so you don't try to lie him.

Keep fit *[Verb + Adjective]* *(to keep your body healthy by exercising regularly.)*

I keep myself fit by doing physical exercises every morning.

Running three or four kilometers a day is a great way for everyone to keep themselves fit.

Keep up with your studies *[Verb + Noun]* *(to make progress or learn at the same level as others.)*

Keep up with your studies or you'll fall behind.

If you want to be a successful student, you must keep up with your studies at college.

Keep one's figure [Verb + Noun] *(to keep or maintain a slim and attractive bodily shape.)*

He exercises regularly to keep his figure.

Alice wants to stay young and keep her figure.

Keep your word [Verb + Noun] *(keep your promise (do what you promised to do))*

Keep your word and give me my money back.

Did peter keep his word to you?

Keep your temper [Verb + Noun] *(to refrain from becoming angry/ to stay calm and not get angry.)*

It's important to keep your temper with the children.

It was hard to keep my temper with so many things going wrong.

Keep in touch = stay in touch (with someone) [Verb + Noun] *(to continue to write or speak to someone by phone, mail, email, etc. Although you do not see them often.)*

Lucy and her ex-husband still keep in touch.

I still keep in touch with all my college roommate, mostly by email.

COLLOCATIONS/L

Lose touch with *[Verb + Noun]* *(to not see or hear from someone any longer/ to no longer see, hear or communicate with someone.)*

John and I were close friends in high school, but when we moved to different colleges, we gradually lost touch with each other.

Peter lost touch with his college roommates after graduation.

I lost touch with Richard after he moved to London.

Lifelong friend *[Adjective + Noun]* *(someone who has been your friend for the whole of your life.)*

He became a lifelong friend of mine.

She has been a lifelong friend of ours.

Long-term relationship *[Adjective + Noun]* *(a relationship that continues a long time in the future.)*

He is 40 and he's never had a long-term relationship.

Mary wishes she had a long-term relationship with the guy she loves.

Lull someone to sleep *[Verb + Noun]* *(to make someone relaxed enough to sleep.)*

The sound of rain falling lulled her to sleep.

The woman lulled her son to sleep on her knees.

The sound of waterfall soon lulled him to sleep.

Luxury hotel *[Adjective + Noun]* *(a hotel which is very comfortable; containing expensive and enjoyable things or services.)*

The luxury hotel charges $150 for one night stay.

We spent 3 days and 4 nights at a local luxury hotel.

Light rain *[Adjective + Noun] (a small amount of rain.)*

A light rain began to fall when we were going outside.

There was a light rain last night, and it made the sidewalks wet.

Lighten someone's workload *[Verb + Noun] (to reduce the amount of work that somebody has.)*

Tom is trying to lighten his workload.

Measures should be taken by schools by cutting down irrelevant subjects in order to lighten students' workload.

Last year she suffered a mild stroke and she was advised to lighten her workload.

Live music *[Adjective + Noun] (music played on instruments in front of an audience.)*

It's hard to find a club which performs live music in this area.

Peter likes to go to a local jazz club where he can enjoy live music.

Leave university *[Verb + Noun] (to stop going to university.)*

My brother left university in 2004.

After he left university, he travelled for 2 months.

Launch a product *[Verb + Noun] (to introduce a new product for sale for the first time to attract attention to it.)*

They always carry out market research before launching a new product.

Launching a new product is an exciting time for any business.

Last long *[Verb + Adverb] (continue or exist for a long period of time.)*

Tom is very kind to me. I hope that our friendship will last long.

If henry keeps being so rude to the customers, his job will not last long.

Late night *[Adjective + Noun]* (*a night when you stay awake until a late hour.*)

Jane looks a bit tired this morning because she had a late night last night.

You've had too many late nights recently, so you should have an early night.

Laugh out loud *[Verb + Adverb]* (*laugh aloud so people can hear you, normally used as a response to something funny.*)

The comedy was so funny that I couldn't help laughing out loud on the bus.

He was trying hard not to laugh out loud.

Cartoons often make us laugh out loud.

Law and order *[Noun + Noun]* (*a situation in which the rules of a society or the laws of a country are being respected and obeyed.*)

Respect and obedience for law and order are the first precepts of any civilized society.

To restore and preserve law and order, the government should arrange 5,000 extra police officers on the streets.'

Lay the groundwork *[Verb + Noun]* (*to do what is necessary at an early stage in preparation for future work.*)

We're busy laying the groundwork for another aid project.

The government is laying the groundwork for future economic growth.

Lead the field = lead the pack *[Verb + Noun]* (*to be in the leading position in a race.*)

John led the field throughout the race.

He didn't win the race although he led the field in the early part of it.

Lead the way *[Verb + Noun]* (*to go first to show others the way to somewhere; to be the best or the first to do something.*)

Henry led the way through the forest, and we followed.

My group of five members walked down toward the beach with the tour guide leading the way.

Our company led the way in developing this new software.

Lead the world [Verb + Noun] (to be the most successful in the world.)

Our country leads the world in the production of oil.

Japan leads the world in the mass production of electronic devices.

Lead to believe [Verb + Verb] (to cause someone to believe something untrue.)

I had been led to believe that if I worked hard, I wouldn't lose my job.

He led me to believe that this product was guaranteed.

Leading role [Adjective + Noun] (the most important role in music, ballet, cinema, theater, etc.)

Michael Douglas was the leading role in a major Hollywood movie.

People tend to see a movie with a star in the leading role.

Leave a message [Verb + Noun] (to leave a piece of written or spoken information for someone you haven't been able to meet or talk to them directly.)

Tom: can I talk to Jane?

Mary: she's not here.

Tom: could I leave a message?

Mary: sure, you can leave a message for her.

Leave home [Verb + Noun] (to stop living with your parents and live in your own home.)

Peter left home when he finished high school.

Joe didn't leave home until she got married.

Leave someone alone = let someone alone [Verb + Adverb] (to stop *bothering, annoying, or criticizing someone.)*

Please leave me alone. I need to concentrate on my study.

I wish my girlfriend would just leave me alone.

Leave school *[Verb + Noun] (to stop going to school or to finish your education.)*

My brother left school when he was 14.

David left school at sixteen and worked as a waiter in a western-style restaurant.

Leave something alone *[Verb + Adverb] (if you leave something alone, you do not touch it, change it or do anything to it.)*

Please leave my book alone – I'm going to read it.

My brother told me to leave his things alone while he was away.

Legal advice *[Adjective + Noun] (professional advice provided by a lawyer, or any other legal experts.)*

If you think she is in breach of contract, don't be afraid to seek legal advice.

I always get legal advice from my lawyer before signing a contract.

Let go *[Verb + Verb] (to allow a person or an animal to go free.)*

The police officer had to let him go due to insufficient evidence.

They let jack go after holding him for over three hours.

He caught a fish and then let it go.

Let go *[Verb + Verb] (to stop holding someone or something.)*

Let go of my hand, you're hurting me!

Don't let the kite go if you want to watch it float up into the sky.

Let someone know *[Verb + Verb] (to tell or inform something to someone.)*

Don't forget to let me know when you arrive home.

Please let me know if you need any assistance.

Level playing field *[Adjective + Noun]* *(a situation in which everyone has an equal opportunity of succeeding.)*

All companies will be provided a level playing field after the government revises the tax code.

If you both started off with a level playing field, your relationship would be far better.

Level teaspoon/tablespoon *[Adjective + Noun]* *(an amount that fills a teaspoon/tablespoon to the level of the sides of the spoon, without going above its edges.)*

The recipe says to add two level teaspoons of sugar and one level teaspoon of salt.

It would be better if you put a level teaspoon of sugar in your coffee.

Lie ahead *[Verb + Adverb]* *(if something lies ahead, it is going to happen in the future (especially something difficult or unpleasant))*

We need to be ready for many challenges lying ahead.

If you get a university degree, a good future lies ahead of you.

Light a fire under somebody *[Verb + Noun]* *(to make someone work better or harder.)*

I tried to light a fire under him when I saw that he didn't work hard.

You ought to light a fire under the mechanic or he'll never finish repairing the car.

Liquid refreshment *[Adjective + Noun]* *(drinks, usually alcoholic drinks.)*

You must be thirsty. Would you like some liquid refreshment?

After a hard day at work, I usually enjoy some liquid refreshment.

Little bit *[Phrase]* *(slightly, or to some extent; a small amount of something.)*

This one is a little bit smaller than that one.

I have a little bit of money left.

Tom needs a little bit of time to finish his essay.

I was a little bit lucky to get that job.

Little brother *[Adjective + Noun]* *(younger brother (a brother who is younger than you))*

My little brother is 5 years younger than I am.

He loves to play games with his little brother at the weekend.

Little sister *[Adjective + Noun]* *(younger sister (a sister who is younger than you))*

Tomorrow is my little sister's birthday, so I need to prepare a special gift for her.

My little sister studies law.

Little known *[Adjective + Noun]* *(not known by a lot of people.)*

He was little known outside of japan.

The word "furusiyya" has been little known outside of the Middle East.

Live at home *[Verb + Noun]* *(to live in the home of your parents.)*

Although Bill is 30 years old, he still lives at home.

I lived at home when I was single.

Living conditions *[Noun + Noun]* *(standard of living.)*

Poor living conditions are linked to fatal diseases.

The government needs to raise awareness and educate people to improve their living conditions.

Long ago *[Adverb + Adverb]* *(in the distant past.)*

My father stopped working as a police officer long ago.

His parents got divorced long ago.

Long overdue [Adverb + Adjective] *(if something is overdue, it should have been done or happened a long time ago.)*

She is long overdue for a medical check-up.

The reform of our political and educational system is long overdue.

Long time [Adjective + Noun] *(a great amount of time; having existed, occurred, or continued for a long period of time.)*

It takes a long time to master a new language.

Tom's recovery has taken him a long time.

Long way [Adjective + Noun] *(a great distance.)*

The beach is a long way (away) from here.

He went a long way to see his girlfriend.

England is a long way from japan.

Look nice [Verb + Adjective] *(to look good (appear attractive, pleasant, enjoyable, delicious, etc.))*

You look very nice with your new haircut.

Those apples look nice. How much is it for one kilo?

Lose a game [Verb + Noun] *(to fail to win or to be defeated in a game.)*

If they lose this game, they will be out of the championship.

He is an excellent tennis player. He hasn't lost many games in this season.

Lose a job [Verb + Noun] *(no longer have your job because it has been taken from you.)*

Bill is a dedicated employee, so I can't believe that he has lost his job.

Although Jane is a hard-working worker, she lost her job.

Lose control *[Verb + Noun] (unable to be in control of something.)*

It's dangerous if you lose control of your car on the roads.

He lost control of his car on a slippery road.

Her father tends to lose control whenever he gets so angry.

Lose faith (in something or someone) *[Verb + Noun] (to no longer believe in someone or something.)*

We have lost faith in bill's ability to manage the restaurant properly.

Jessica lost faith in her religion and became an atheist.

Lose hope *[Verb + Noun] (to no longer believe that something might be possible.)*

He'd lost hope of winning the game, so he was defeated easily.

Peter had lost hope of ever being promoted, so he quit his job.

Lose interest *[Verb + Noun] (to stop being interested in something.)*

After losing interest in accounting, Joe quit her job and became a fashion designer.

The film was so boring, so john lost interest and started playing games on his phone.

Lose money *[Verb + Noun] (to earn less money than you spend after gambling, investing, starting a business, etc.)*

My brother's company has been losing money for the past two years, and he is getting really worried.

Her husband has lost all their money on gambling.

Lose weight *[Verb + Noun] (if you lose weight, you become lighter.)*

Jane lost five pounds in weight during her time in the hospital.

My sister is a bit overweight, so she's trying to lose weight.

Lose your life [Verb + Noun] (to die suddenly because of an accident, war, illness, etc.)

Hundreds of people lost their lives in the floods.

He lost his life in a car accident.

Lose your temper [Verb + Noun] (to suddenly become very angry.)

Her husband lost his temper and started shouting at her.

I've never seen my father lose his temper.

Love dearly [Verb + Adverb] (to love very much.)

I love my little brother dearly.

Lucy loves her parents dearly.

Carol loves her husband dearly despite all his faults.

Loved one [Adjective + Noun] (someone who you love, especially a member of your family or your partner.)

Many of my friends and loved ones visited bill at his house.

I and my loved ones are going to take a trip to Europe next month.

The doctors allowed his loved ones to see him, but his friends had to wait outside.

Lucky escape [Adjective + Noun] (to avoid being killed or badly injured simply because you are lucky.)

A married couple had a lucky escape when a big tree fell just in front of their house.

It was a serious accident, but he had a lucky escape and was still alive.

Large size [Adjective + Noun] (a bigger size than average (of clothing, goods, etc.))

My husband is quite fat, so I'd like to exchange this t-shirt for the large size.

Do you have any sweater in the large size?

Lonely place *[Adjective + Noun]* *(a remote place where very few people come.)*

They live in a very lonely place on the top of the mountain.

Do you know what he is doing in such a lonely place?

Lie in ruins = be in ruin *[Verb + Noun]* *(if a building or an area lies in ruins, it has been badly damaged or destroyed.)*

The old castle lay in ruins in 1982.

The ancient town lay in ruins after the war and was rebuilt with distinctive architecture.

Local crafts *[Adjective + Noun]* *(work or objects produced locally by hand.)*

We displayed our products at the local crafts fair.

My parents used to produce and sell local crafts.

Long weekend *[Adjective + Noun]* *(a weekend holiday which is extended by one or two extra days including Friday or Monday.)*

We went to New York for a long weekend.

Joe spent a long weekend with her parents in the countryside.

Learn something by heart *[Phrase]* *(to memorize something so well that you can write or recite it exactly.)*

The director told john to learn his speech by heart.

The teacher asked all students to learn this poem by heart.

Low-budget film *[Adjective + Noun]* *(a film which is made or produced with a small amount of money.)*

It was an extremely low-budget film.

They are currently producing a low-budget film.

Lose one's temper *[Verb + Noun]* *(to suddenly become very angry at someone or something.)*

Her boss lost his temper and began shouting at her.

My mom lost her temper and yelled at me.

Launch a product *[Verb + Noun]* *(to start selling a new product to the public.)*

If you want to be successful, you need to put your best effort when you launch a new product.

Our company is going to launch a new product in January.

Look young for your age *[Phrase]* *(to behave or seem as though someone is younger than he/she really is.)*

Lucy is a nice girl, but she looks very young for her age.

Bill is fed up with people always telling him that he looks young for his age.

If anyone tells you that you look young for your age then show them your real age with your maturity.

Lose one's figure *[Verb + Noun]* *(to fail to keep or maintain a slim and attractive bodily shape.)*

She is a modern girl - she doesn't want to lose her figure.

She might lose her figure after giving birth to children.

She loses her figure since she has eaten too much fast food recently.

Lively bars/restaurants *[Adjective + Noun]* *(bars or restaurants that are full of activity and excitement.)*

It was a lively bar with good live music.

This lively restaurant serves Italian food at reasonable prices.

Live music *[Adjective + Noun]* *(a live performance is given in front of an audience.)*

Peter usually goes to his favorite bar to enjoy live music on Saturday nights.

Watching live music is a great way to refresh myself.

Long-range weather forecast *[Adjective + Noun]* (the weather forecast made for a long period of time ahead.)

The long-range weather forecast predicts sunny days.

The great news is that the long-range weather forecast is fine for this summer.

Local shops *[Adjective + Noun]* (shops that belong to a certain place or district.)

These local shops are very good for local people.

We went to many local shops last week.

Loyalty card *[Noun + Noun]* (a plastic card that is given to a regular customer by a shop or a business to reward them for buying goods or services such as price reductions.)

I picked up a loyalty card from this store last week.

Have you collected a loyalty card from Gloria jean's coffees store?

Long-term investment *[Adjective + Noun]* (any investment that someone holds for a long term period.)

Our most important long-term investment is education.

My long-term investment includes real estate, stocks, and bonds.

Low-risk investment *[Adjective + Noun]* (an investment that is considered to be relatively safe, just a small chance of losing all of your money.)

Buying a corporate bond is supposed to be a very good and low-risk investment opportunity.

He continues to view debt funds as a very low-risk investment opportunity.

Long-term solution *[Adjective + Noun]* (a solution that will be effective for a long time.)

The local authority is working to find long-term solutions for the homeless.

The government is working to find long-term solutions for environmental problems.

Long sandy beach [Adjective + Noun] *(a long beach that is covered with sand.)*

We were walking on a long sandy beach.

We met at a long sandy beach called a crescent beach.

Language barrier [Noun + Noun] *(a difficulty for people communicating with each other because they are unable to speak a common language.)*

Alice wasn't able to enjoy herself in Chinese because of the language barrier.

Tom hopes to be able to overcome the language barrier when he moves to Madrid.

Low-cost airline [Adjective + Noun] *(an airline that offers passenger flights at very low prices and fewer comforts.)*

Air Asia is supposed to be an extremely low-cost airline.

Do you like to use a low-cost airline for a business trip?

She is finding a low-cost airline ticket so she can visit her grandmother.

Long-distance travel [Adjective + Noun] *(the activity of travelling a long way.)*

Long-distance travel usually causes drowsiness.

Long-distance travel is usually cheaper, but it is not very fast or comfortable.

Lay off staff [Verb + Noun] *(to temporarily or permanently terminate someone's job because of a shortage of work.)*

The company has laid off more than 50 staff.

The hotel laid off fifteen staff since the number of tourists decreased.

Lose one's patience [Verb + Noun] *(if you lose your patience, you are unable to* *keep your temper, and become suddenly angry.)*

He lost his patience and decided to attack the young man.

The woman lost her patience and assaulted the boy.

Long-lasting friendship *[Adjective + Noun] (a friendship continuing for a long period of time.)*

Tom does not usually make big mistakes with Alice. They have a long-lasting friendship.

Peter's had a long-lasting friendship with Susan since they were in high school.

Love at first sight *[Phrase] (a love which is established as soon as two people first see each other.)*

Do you believe in love at first sight?

When john saw Susan at the party, he knew it was love at first sight. He immediately believed that she was the one for him.

Love each other unconditionally *[Verb + Adverb] (to love each other without any conditions or requirements.)*

Jack and rose love each other unconditionally with their hearts.

They loved each other unconditionally even when they parted ways.

Let someone down *[Phrase] (to make someone disappointed by failing to support or help them as they are expecting you to do.)*

Don't worry, she won't let you down.

When he forgot to get his mom from the airport, he let her down.

Peter broke up with his girlfriend because she was always letting him down.

Lucrative job *[Adjective + Noun] (a job where someone earns a lot of money.)*

He has a lucrative job offer in California.

Her parents want her to marry a guy with a lucrative job – like a lawyer or doctor.

Lodge a complaint *[Verb + Noun] (to make a formal complaint about something.)*

He intends to lodge a complaint against the police.

She walked into the office to lodge a complaint against the company.

COLLOCATIONS/M

Meet basic human needs *[Phrase] (to meet the elements required for survival, such as food, water, shelter, etc.)*

A high income allows people to meet their basic human needs.

We are providing children and communities with food, clothing, toys, soap, and other essential items to help them meet their basic human needs.

Make something a reality *[Verb + Noun] (to make something real/ make something happen/ make something possible.)*

He's made his dream to be a billionaire a reality.

She's made her dream to be a doctor a reality.

Mental agility *[Adjective + Noun] (ability to think rapidly and clearly.)*

Her mental agility has never been in doubt.

His mental agility allowed him to follow both conversations at once.

Maintain quality *[Verb + Noun] (to make something continue at the same quality.)*

We always try to maintain quality of our services.

In order to maintain quality of their products, they only use the finest raw material to produce.

Meet a target *[Verb + Noun] (to achieve a target.)*

He's been working hard to meet his targets this year.

The government has been trying to meet their targets for domestic energy conservation.

Master vital soft skills *[Phrase] (to master important skills that enable someone to communicate well with other people.)*

Nowadays, employees and students find it hard to master vital soft skills, such as teamwork, communications, and emotional intelligence.

A majority of young people have difficulties in mastering vital soft skills.

Manage conflicts [Verb + Noun] *(limit the negative aspects of conflict while increasing the positive aspects of conflict.)*

There are many ways on how to manage conflicts and disagreements.

A lot of employers find it hard to manage conflicts between employees.

More and more dependent on [Phrase] *(increasingly addicted to something.)*

Youngsters are more and more dependent on electronic products and social networks on the Internet.

People are more and more dependent on cell phones and the Internet.

Make the/ an effort (to do something) [Phrase] *(to try hard to do or get something.)*

You must study and make an effort if you want to pass your exams.

You won't get lonely if you make an effort to see people

Make a mistake [Verb + Noun] *(to do something that's wrong or has bad results.)*

He promised he wouldn't make the same mistake again!

Susan usually learns from the mistakes she has made.

Make a decision [Verb + Noun] *(to decide what to do.)*

He made a decision to study overseas.

We haven't made a decision about where to go on holiday yet.

Make way (for somebody/something) [Phrase] *(to allow someone/something to pass; to be replaced by somebody or something.)*

They were asked to make way for the bride and groom.

Most of the old buildings have made way for restaurants and shopping centres.

Make demands on *[Phrase]* *(to cause problems for someone or something; urgently require something of someone.)*

Her father's illness has made considerable demands on her time.

Enforcing the current law is making ridiculous demands on police.

Meet the requirements (for something) *[Verb + Noun]* *(to fulfill the requirements for something.)*

I think mark will be able to meet the requirements for the job.

His skills did not meet the requirements for this position.

Make progress *[Verb + Noun]* *(to get closer to a goal, or to improve in ability.)*

Susan is making progress in learning Japanese.

He is making progress in his profession.

Make an impression on somebody *[Phrase]* *(to make someone notice and admire you; to produce a positive memorable effect on somebody.)*

Tom made quite an impression on the girls at the dance club.

Peter certainly made an impression on Mary.

Major problem *[Adjective + Noun]* *(very big problem.)*

Traffic congestion in big cities continues to be a major problem.

Illegal immigration seems to be a major problem in America.

MAKE

Make arrangements for *[Verb + Noun]* *(to prepare or arrange all aspects of an event such as a wedding, funeral, meeting, conference, etc. So that it can happen.)*

They'd made all the arrangements for the wedding.

Most of the arrangements for the conference have already been made.

Make a change/changes *[Verb + Noun] (to make something different from how it was and therefore it is likely to be interesting, enjoyable, etc.)*

It makes a change to see her smiling.

Mark made necessary changes after reading the teacher's comments on his essays.

Make a comment/comments *[Verb + Noun] (to express an opinion about something.)*

Her mom always makes comments on what she is wearing.

Please make a comment on our website.

Make a contribution to *[Verb + Noun] (to help produce or achieve something together with other people, or to help make something successful.)*

This invention made a major contribution to science.

Local police have made a significant contribution to crime prevention.

Make a decision *[Verb + Noun] (to decide what to do.)*

He has to make his decision by next week.

The company will make a decision shortly.

Make an effort *[Verb + Noun] (to put time and energy into doing something even though you do not want to or you find it difficult.)*

I wish he would make an effort to get on with his girlfriend.

Peter is obviously making a special effort to be nice to his wife at the present.

Make an excuse/ make excuses *[Verb + Noun] (to give false reasons to explain why you do something or why you cannot do something.)*

Mark is always making excuses for not helping peter.

David got to work late and made some excuses about being stuck in the traffic.

Make friends [Verb + Noun] *(to form new friendships; to become a friend of someone.)*

Julie made a lot of new friends at college.

We made friends with the children next door.

Make a mistake [Verb + Noun] *(to do something that's wrong or has bad results.)*

She admitted that she had made a mistake.

She made a mistake of giving him her phone number.

Make a phone call [Verb + Noun] *(to telephone someone.)*

I have to make a few phone calls before the meeting.

I need to make a phone call before breakfast.

Make progress [Verb + Noun] *(to get closer to a goal, or to improve or develop in skills, knowledge, etc.)*

The English course allows students to make progress at their own speed.

Julie is making much progress with her Spanish.

Make strides [Verb + Noun] *(to make progress towards a goal.)*

They are making great strides in the search for a cure.

Mark and David made strides to expand their business internationally.

Make a bed [Verb + Noun] *(to arrange the sheets, blankets, and pillows on a bed so that they are tidy)*

Lucy hurried upstairs and quickly made her bed before going to work.

Tom nearly always remembers to make his bed before he leaves for school.

Make a difference [Verb + Noun] *(to have an important effect on a situation or something, especially a good effect).*

The increase of living costs would make a big difference to our quality of life.

Changing schools made a big difference to her life.

Make a fortune [Verb + Noun] *(to make a large amount of money, goods, property, etc.)*

My brother made a fortune in real estate.

They made a fortune from mining.

He has made a huge fortune from his novels.

Make a mess [Verb + Noun] *(to make something look dirty or untidy; to create an untidy or disorganized state or situation)*

Jane makes a terrible mess when she's cooking.

The kids made a mess in the bedroom.

Make a reservation = make a booking [Verb + Noun] *(to book or reserve a seat on a plane or train, a table in a restaurant, a room in a hotel, etc. To be kept for you)*

She called the restaurant and made a reservation.

I'd like to make a table reservation for three people at 7 p.m.

Can I make a booking for Saturday?

Make an appointment [Verb + Noun] *(to arrange a date and time to meet or visit somebody at a particular time, especially for a reason connected with their work)*

I would like to make an appointment with Dr. Stephens, please.

If you want to see Mr. Johnson, you'll have to make an appointment first. He is very busy now.

Make an offer [Verb + Noun] *(to officially state a particular price that you would like to pay for something)*

Did he make you an offer for the house?

Mark has made an offer on a house in New York.

Make believe *[verb + verb] (to pretend or imagine that something is real or true)*

The kids like to make believe that they are kings and queens.

Since Julie didn't want to make her boyfriend hurt, so she made believe that everything was fine.

Make clear *[verb + adjective] (to make something easy to understand, or to express yourself clearly)*

Could you please make clear this point?

Could you make yourself clear why you are going to quit your job?

Make contact *[Verb + Noun] (to communicate with somebody, for example by telephone or letter, etc.)*

Diana has been calling her boyfriend for weeks but she still hasn't made contact.

Thanks to the internet, people find it easier to make contact with their old friends whom they don't often meet in person.

Make love *[Verb + Noun] (to have sex with someone that you love)*

That was the first time they made love.

Not all people want to have a baby when they make love.

Make room (for someone or something) *[Verb + Noun] (to give room or to provide space for someone or something by moving other things)*

Make room for Lucy. She needs a place to sit.

I need to move some of the furniture to make room for the refrigerator.

Make sb feel sth *[verb + verb] (to cause somebody to feel a certain way)*

It makes him feel good to know his work is appreciated.

The smell of cigarette makes me feel sick.

Make sense [Verb + Noun] *(to be clear and easy to understand)*

The last paragraph of the essay doesn't make any sense.

Everything she said entirely made sense.

Make something easy [verb + adjective] **(to cause something to be less difficult)**

The internet makes it really easy for people to find music, videos, or do research online.

Computers make our jobs easier.

Make sure = make certain [verb + adjective] *(to check something so that you can be sure about it)*

He looked around to make sure that he was alone.

Make sure tom is honest before you give him the car.

Main course [Adjective + Noun] *(the largest or most important part of a meal.)*

We had salmon and vegetables for our main course.

After the main course, we have dessert.

Main road [Adjective + Noun] *(a large and important road with lots of traffic that leads from one town or city to another.)*

Our fashion shop is on the main road out of town.

His parents didn't allow him to ride a bike on main roads.

Main thing [Adjective + Noun] *(the most important thing.)*

At least he wasn't injured in the accident. That's the main thing.

If you don't get the job, the main thing is to never give up hope.

Make a bed [Verb + Noun] *(to arrange the sheets and covers on a bed so that they are tidy.)*

Mom asked me to make my bed before I left for school.

Julie makes her bed every morning.

Make a decision *[Verb + Noun] (to decide what to do after thinking carefully.)*

Bill made a decision to quit his job since he found it so boring.

My brother made a poor decision when he dropped out of school.

Make a fuss *[Verb + Noun] (to create unnecessary anger, worry, concern or excitement about something.)*

The boy made such a fuss when his mom spilled a drop of milk on his t-shirt!

Tom felt so ashamed of himself for making such a fuss.

Make a mistake *[Verb + Noun] (to do something wrong; to do something that has bad results.)*

He promised he wouldn't make the same mistake again!

We've learnt a lot from the mistakes we've made.

Make a note (of) = take a note (of) *[Verb + Noun] (to write something down so as to remember.)*

I made a note of his name and address. I will call him tomorrow.

Did you make a note of the car's number?

Make amends *[Verb + Noun] (to do something to show you're sorry for a mistake that you have made or a bad situation that you have caused.)*

Bill tried to make amends to his girlfriend for his bad behavior.

He tried to make amends by apologizing and returning the cell phone he had stolen.

Make an effort *[Verb + Noun] (to attempt to do something you find it difficult.)*

You'll be able to master a language within a short period of time if you make an effort.

He hasn't had a girlfriend since he hasn't made an effort with girls.

Make an excuse *[Verb + Noun]* *(to create a reason to explain why you have done something bad, or for not doing something you should do.)*

Tom's always making excuses for his bad behaviour.

What excuse did he make for being so late?

Make arrangements *[Verb + Noun]* *(to plan or prepare for an event such as a wedding, funeral, meeting, conference, etc.)*

We are making all the arrangements for the wedding.

All the arrangements for the party have already been made.

Make progress *[Verb + Noun]* *(to continue to develop or move forward in one's work or activity.)*

My sister is making much progress with her Japanese.

Peter is making progress in English.

Married couple *[Adjective + Noun]* *(two people who are married to each other.)*

Are jack and Mary a married couple? No, they are just good colleagues.

Eighteen young married couples were involved in the survey.

A young married couple moved into the vacant apartment yesterday.

Mass market *[Adjective + Noun]* *(the market for goods that are produced and distributed in large quantities and appeal to a large number of consumers.)*

Mobile technologies have accessed to the mass market of japan.

Science fiction and fantasy paperbacks have hit the mass market.

May (very) well *[Verb + Adverb]* *(be likely to happen or be true.)*

What she said may very well be true.

I'm free this morning, but I may very well busy this afternoon.

Medical care *[Adjective + Noun]* *(professional treatment for someone who's sick or injured by a doctor, nurse, or other healthcare professional.)*

Many people died due to the lack of proper medical care.

Children without medical care are often less healthy.

Medical history *[Adjective + Noun]* *(a record of past medical problems and treatments that someone has had in the past.)*

The doctor asked about his mother's medical history.

Your medical history will decide the sort of treatment.

Meet a need *[Verb + Noun]* *(to satisfy the need; to provide what is needed.)*

This school is popular because it meets the needs of all our children.

We haven't found an apartment that meets our needs.

Meet a target *[Verb + Noun]* *(to achieve a target.)*

Several countries have not met their targets for energy conservation.

Our team will get a cash bonus if we meet our sales targets.

Meet opposition *[Verb + Noun]* *(to get a bad result or reaction.)*

A new tax would meet strong opposition from the public.

The fact that he left home met strong opposition from his parents.

Meet with approval *[Verb + Noun]* *(to receive a positive response or reaction/ to be acceptable to someone; to be approved of by someone.)*

Jane's boyfriend failed to meet with her father's approval.

Does the quality of the service meet with your approval?

Mental illness *[Adjective + Noun]* *(a condition which causes serious disorder in a person's normal state of mind.)*

There is an increasing number of people who have suffered from depression, addictions and mental illnesses nowadays.

Many college students have been diagnosed with some sort of mental illness.

Miles away *[Phrase] (a long way away from a particular place.)*

We will be exhausted if we walk to the beach. It's miles away.

The shopping mall is not miles away. It's only about 1 kilometer away from my house.

Miss a flight *[Verb + Noun] (to arrive too late to board a flight.)*

Tom overslept at the airport and missed his flight.

We went to the airport too late, and we missed our flight.

Miss an opportunity = miss a chance *[Verb + Noun] (to fail to take advantage of an opportunity or a chance to do something.)*

If I have an opportunity to meet the president, I won't miss it.

Tom didn't miss a chance of promotion when he accepted the job of marketing director.

Missing in action *[Adjective + Noun] (if someone is "missing in action", they haven't been seen, contacted or confirmed as either alive or dead.)*

Nearly 100 soldiers are listed as missing in action.

Her brother and her husband had been missing in action for more than 10 years.

Mixed feelings = mixed emotions *[Adjective + Noun] (conflicting feelings or emotions about something or someone (you can see both good and bad points about them))*

I have mixed feelings about the horror film, excited and scared at the same time.

Bob has mixed feelings about his girlfriend. Sometimes he thinks she loves him; other times he doesn't.

Moral obligation *[Adjective + Noun]* (something that you must do because you know it is morally right.)

It is necessary that all people must have a moral obligation to defend human rights.

I think we should have a moral obligation to help children who are disabled.

More or less *[Adverb + Adverb]* (almost; approximately.)

Jack became more or less familiar with the cold weather.

The box is very heavy. I guess it's 60 kilos, more or less.

Murder mystery *[Noun + Noun]* (a detective story book, play or film about a narrative of a murder and how the murderer is discovered.)

My father is quite into murder mysteries.

He is a great author who has written over 30 murder mysteries.

Mysterious circumstances *[Adjective + Noun]* (circumstances that aren't understood, or known, or explained.)

A group of five men disappeared under mysterious circumstances.

He died in mysterious circumstances. No-one knows what happened to him.

Main meal *[Adjective + Noun]* (the meal of the day at which you eat the most food.)

Dinner is our main meal of the day.

Lunch is usually our main meal, except on Saturdays and Sundays.

Make someone's mouth water *[Verb + Noun]* (to make someone want to eat something immediately since it smells or looks so good.)

The smell of the bacon and eggs made his mouth water.

Just thinking about the cooked fish made her mouth water.

Mature student [Adjective + Noun] *(a student who begins studying at a college or university at an older age than usual.)*

He studied at the college as a mature student.

She is 24 years old, so she is eligible to apply as a mature student.

Master's degree [Noun + Noun] *(an advanced academic degree that is awarded by a college or university to a student who has studied a subject for about one or two years beyond the bachelor's degree.)*

I got a master's degree in education two years ago.

He is pursuing a master's degree in chemical engineering.

Meet a deadline [Verb + Noun] *(to finish a job or task by or before it is due/ to finish something in time.)*

He is working extremely hard to meet a deadline.

I'm afraid we won't be able to meet our deadline.

Manual work [Adjective + Noun] *(work that involves your physical strength, usually using your hands rather than your mind.)*

My mom really enjoys sewing. It is manual work.

Do you like doing manual work?

Mobile home [Adjective + Noun] *(a type of small building that is built in a factory and then moved to the place where people will live in it.)*

It's a beautiful mobile home!

They are planning to have a mobile home built next week.

Mix and match [Phrase] *(to choose different things such as clothing or pieces of equipment and put them together to form a coordinated set.)*

Susan learned to mix and match her sweaters with different skirts and blouses to create new outfits.

Sarah usually buys clothing that she can mix and match.

Make a profit *[Verb + Noun]* (*to make money from business, investments or by selling things, especially the money that remains after paying the costs involved*)

David bought the house for $200,000 and sold it for $250,000, so he made a profit of $50,000.

They make a big profit from selling office equipment to local companies.

Massive hit *[Adjective + Noun]* (*if a record, film, book, or play is a massive hit, it is very successful and popular.*)

The film/song became a massive hit in 1995.

Danielle steel's book is a massive hit and has made her name around the world.

Music festival *[Noun + Noun]* (*an entertainment event including a lot of music performances, typically lasting several days.*)

We are now preparing for the music festival next month.

Would you like to go to the music festival with me?

Mild climate *[Adjective + Noun]* (*a climate that is not very cold or severe, and therefore pleasant.*)

We love to live in a mild climate.

Our city has a mild climate. It seldom snows here.

The mild climate here lets people enjoy outdoor activities like playing football, swimming, running and picnicking all year round.

Mild winter *[Adjective + Noun]* (*winter that is not extremely cold.*)

Our city is famous for its very mild winter climate.

We had a very mild winter last year, with almost no snow.

Must-have product *[Adjective + Noun]* (*a product that many people want to have.*)

For most people, a mobile phone is a must-have product.

The latest version of the software is a must-have for professionals.

Man-made disaster *[Adjective + Noun] (an unexpected event caused by the action of humans that results in a lot of damage or kills a lot of people.)*

The devastating landslide was a man-made disaster.

The nuclear accident in japan was a man-made disaster.

Mailing list *[Noun + Noun] (a list of names and contact details kept by an organization so that it can send information and advertisements by post or electronic mail.)*

He has included me on his mailing list for future workshops.

Could you please add my email address to your mailing list?

Mass media *[Noun + Noun] (the means of communication that reach great numbers of people, such as newspapers, popular magazines, television, and radio.)*

There are a variety of mass media nowadays.

Television, newspapers, magazines and radio are called the mass media.

Must-read book *[Adjective + Noun] (a book is so useful that it should or must be read.)*

This is a must-read book about crime for law students.

The teacher gave his students a must-read book list.

Must-see movie *[Adjective + Noun] (a movie that is highly recommended as worth seeing.)*

It is the must-see movie of the year.

"Loving in black and white" is a must-see movie.

Make huge profit *[Verb + Noun] (to make a large amount of money in business after paying the costs involved.)*

Our company made huge profit from the overseas market last year.

They made huge profit by selling petroleum products.

Minimum starting salary *[Adjective + Noun]* *(the smallest amount of money that an employee is paid when starting a particular job for the first time.)*

All apprentices are employed and receive a minimum starting salary of $500.

Well-qualified teachers will receive a minimum starting salary of $100,000 – $150,000 per year.

Make a payment *[Verb + Noun]* *(to pay an amount of money.)*

I used a credit card to make a payment.

He has to make a payment of £100 on her debt every month.

You can make a payment in any bank.

Receive a payment *[Verb + Noun]* *(to receive or to be paid an amount of money.)*

I received a payment from a customer yesterday.

He received a payment directly into his bank account.

Monthly payment *[Verb + Noun]* *(the amount a person is required to pay each month until their debt is paid off.)*

His monthly payment for a loan was $320.

She wishes to limit her monthly payment to $250 for a period of three years.

Maximize profit *[Verb + Noun]* *(to increase profit as much as possible.)*

The main function of our company is to maximize profit.

The business executives' duty is to maximize profit.

Minimize cost *[Verb + Noun]* *(to reduce cost to the smallest amount.)*

You must minimize cost if you want to maximize profit.

Our company's objective is to minimize cost.

Money laundering [Noun + Noun] *(the act or practice of concealing the origins of illegally obtained money.)*

He was convicted of drug trafficking and money laundering.

The man who was charged with money laundering faces a sentence of 12 years in jail.

Maintain a hobby [Verb + Noun] *(to continue to be involved in an activity that you enjoy doing/ to keep a hobby.)*

He wants to maintain a hobby of creating websites for others.

She plans to maintain a hobby of interior design.

Mental well-being [Adjective + Noun] *(the state of being mentally healthy.)*

Emotional well-being also has a great effect on our physical health.

He finds it difficult to maintain his positive mental well-being from time to time.

Modern medicine [Adjective + Noun] *(medicine based on science.)*

The baby survived thanks to modern medicine.

He'd be dead right now if it wasn't for modern medicine.

Muscular man [Adjective + Noun] *(a man who is very fit and strong, and has firm muscles.)*

Her husband is a large muscular man.

The muscular man lifted the heavy table and moved it into the kitchen.

Municipal solid waste [Adjective + Noun] *(waste from households.)*

There is an increasing in the amount of municipal solid waste in this area.

The amount of daily municipal solid waste generation has increased dramatically in many big cities recently.

Meet admissions criteria [Verb + Noun] *(to meet the overall procedure and* criteria to get permission to become a student at a college or university.)

Only 15% of applicants meet admissions criteria for top universities.

Any student who meets admissions criteria established by this college will be accepted as non-thesis.

Make a living *[Verb + Noun]* *(to earn money to buy the things you need in life)*

My uncle makes a living as a freelance photographer.

Most young people like to make a living in big cities

Maternity leave *[Noun + Noun]* *(a period of paid absence from work granted to a woman during the months immediately before and after she gives birth.)*

Cheryl will start her maternity leave tomorrow.

My sister will return from maternity leave next week.

Make a fool out of someone *[Phrase]* *(try to make someone seem stupid by deceiving or tricking them.)*

I felt that jack had made a complete fool out of you.

Are you trying to make a fool out of me?

Mutual friends *[Adjective + Noun]* *(friends that you have in common with someone else.)*

We are classmates, so we have many mutual friends.

Mary and peter didn't see any mutual friends at the party.

Make yourself at home *[Phrase]* *(to relax and make yourself comfortable in the same way as you do in your own home.)*

Make yourself at home while I am away.

Come in and make yourself at home. I have something to do now.

Make a list *[Verb + Noun]* *(to include or write things in a list.)*

Could you please make a list of the newly published books?

She always makes a list of items she needs to buy before she goes to the supermarket.

Make a speech *[Adjective + Noun]* *(to give a formal talk to an audience.)*

She is always nervous when she makes a speech.

Tom was asked to make a speech at the meeting last Monday.

Make an early start *[Verb + Noun]* *(to get started on an activity or a journey very early in the day.)*

They are going to make an early start so that they won't get stuck in the traffic.

We want to make an early start tomorrow to avoid the worst of the traffic.

Make a start *[Verb + Noun]* *(to begin doing something.)*

She arrived home and made a start on cleaning the house.

My son can make a start on building his toys.

Make an assumption *[Verb + Noun]* *(to make a decision based on poor evidence.)*

Don't make assumptions about who he is if you have no clue.

Sometimes it's not true when we make assumptions based on what we see.

Make a choice *[Verb + Noun]* *(to choose; to select; to separate and take in preference.)*

If I had to make a choice between higher pay and job security, I'd prefer to choose job security.

Mary was forced to make a choice between her family and her career.

Make a point of something *[Verb + Noun]* *(to give your attention to something to make sure that you will do it.)*

Tom makes a point of treating his employees fairly.

Lucy makes a point of doing exercise every day.

I make a point of calling my mother every two days.

Make a note of something *[Verb + Noun] (to write down something as a reminder so that you don't forget it.)*

Sarah's made a note of the book's title.

Tom made a note of Mary's address and phone number.

Make a suggestion = offer a suggestion *[Verb + Noun] (to offer an idea or a plan for someone to consider or think about.)*

John offered some suggestions for improvements.

He made some suggestions for how to solve the problems effectively.

Would you like to make a suggestion?

Make an apology *[Verb + Noun] (to say sorry for something or a problem that you have done or caused.)*

He made a formal apology for his carelessness.

He'd like to make a public apology for his actions last night

Make a habit of *[Verb + Noun] (if you make a habit of doing something, you begin to do it regularly.)*

My mom's made a habit of going to bed early.

She makes a habit of walking every day.

Make an attempt to *[Verb + Noun] (to make an effort to do something.)*

I made an attempt to swim across the lake.

He made an attempt to be friendly and nice to clients at his job as instructed.

Make a success of (something) *[Verb + Noun] (to make something be successful.)*

Tom's determined to make a success of his business.

She's determined to make a success of her career.

Make someone's acquaintance [Verb + Noun] *(to meet someone for the first time.)*

I was fortunate to make her acquaintance.

Tom made her acquaintance at a business conference.

Make a proposal [Verb + Noun] *(to make a suggestion to someone to consider.)*

He made a proposal to start a business.

She made a proposal to solve our problem.

COLLOCATIONS/N

Narrow the generation gap *[Phrase] (to make the generation gap become smaller.)*

What would be the best way to narrow the generation gap?

Watching entertainment programs provides family members a great way to narrow the generation gap.

Nurture essential skills *[Phrase] (to help a person to develop their necessary skills)*

Watching sci-fi movies is a good method of education to **nurture essential skills** for students.

Watching television is supposed to be a good method of education to nurture essential skills for youngsters.

Children can nurture essential skills by getting involved in one of our summer programs.

Nasty habit *[Adjective + Noun] (a bad or unpleasant habit.)*

Susan has a nasty habit of biting her fingernails.

Joe has a nasty habit of staying in bed late.

Bill has a nasty habit of smoking too much.

Native country *[Adjective + Noun] (the country in which someone is born.)*

Although David has been living in Canada for over 30 years, it isn't his native country. In fact, he was born in England.

They made their way home to their native country, Brazil.

Native speaker *[Adjective + Noun] (someone who has spoken a particular language as their first or native language.)*

They are native speakers of Japanese.

Mark knows he'll never speak Spanish like a native speaker.

Natural causes [Adjective + Noun] *(if someone dies of natural causes, they die naturally because they are ill or old, rather than because of an accident, murder or suicide.)*

His father died of natural causes.

Mr. Lee died from natural causes

Natural resources [Adjective + Noun] *(the natural wealth of a country, consisting of land, oil, coal, rivers, lakes, trees, forests, etc. That has economic value.)*

We have limited natural resources, so we need to conserve them.

Australia is a very wealthy country with large amounts of natural resources.

Neat and tidy [Adjective + Adjective] *(clean and organized, not messy.)*

Jane's house looks very neat and tidy.

My mom likes everything neat and tidy.

My daughter likes to keep her desk neat and tidy.

Need badly = badly need [Verb + Adverb] *(to need something very much.)*

He needs badly more time to study English.

After a hard year at work, we badly need a vacation.

Nervous wreck [Adjective + Noun] *(a person who's extremely worried, stressed or nervous about something.)*

After one week of working for that company, tom was a nervous wreck.

Jane was a nervous wreck before her driving test.

Net profit [Adjective + Noun] *(the actual profit remaining after subtracting all costs from gross receipts.)*

Our company reported a net profit of over 5 million dollars this year.

If the company's net profit increases this year, each employee will get a bonus.

Never knew [Adverb + Verb] (to not know something and be slightly surprised by it.)

I never knew peter was living in London. I thought he was living in Moscow.

I never knew that Lucy was married. I thought she was single.

New generation [Adjective + Noun] (a new group of products, usually technical ones that are all at the same stage of development.)

A new generation of portable computers.

There are many useful applications on our new generation of mobile phones such as video calling, games, music player, etc.

Next-door neighbours [Adjective + Noun] (people living in the next house, apartment, room, etc.)

Peter is my next-door neighbor.

My new next-door neighbours will come over my house for dinner tonight.

Non-stop flight [Adjective + Noun] (a flight made without intermediate stops on its way to a destination.)

I want to save my time, so a non-stop flight will be my preference.

US airways operate non-stop flights between Los Angeles and Toronto every weekend.

Not necessarily [Adverb + Adverb] (not always or not certainly.)

"Buying an apartment will be cheaper than buying a house." "Not necessarily."

Her husband won't necessarily understand why she is going to quit her job.

Nothing else [Phrase] (no more; not anything else.)

If nothing else, the party will be held tomorrow evening.

Last night, my house was robbed. The theft got my phone and my iPad, but nothing else was stolen.

Nothing much = not much *[Phrase]* *(nothing that's important or interesting.)*

There was nothing much to play.

I asked bob what he was stolen and he said, "nothing much."

Nothing wrong with *[Phrase]* *(not anything that causes a problem.)*

Peter and I are very close to each other. There's nothing wrong with our friendship.

The doctor said there was nothing wrong with my mother. She was fine.

Nowhere near *[Adverb + Adverb]* *(not nearly, far away from; not almost, or not similar to.)*

Bill has nowhere near enough money to buy a flat.

The zoo is nowhere near here, so we'll have to take the taxi.

The house has been being built for about 8 years, and it is nowhere near finished.

Null and void *[Noun + Noun]* *(having no legal force; invalidity.)*

The rich man's will was declared null and void since it had been unsigned.

The contract was deemed null and void because the service wasn't delivered on time.

Navigate a website *[Verb + Noun]* *(to successfully find your way around a website by using the links contained in it.)*

I helped bill navigate a website to look for the information he wanted.

Navigating a website successfully and efficiently is very important these days.

Nine-to-five job *[Adjective + Noun]* *(a job with normal office hours, usually from nine o'clock until five o'clock.)*

I don't like working a nine-to-five job. I prefer to be self-employed.

Tom is tired of working a nine-to-five job. He likes the freedom, and he wants to be his own boss.

Niche market *[Noun + Noun]* *(a small, specialized market for a particular product or service in which there is a limited number of customers.)*

Our product has a niche market and it will take some time for us to find customers.

Teenagers are our niche market.

Natural disaster *[Adjective + Noun]* *(a natural event such as a flood, earthquake, or hurricane that causes great damage or loss of life.)*

Almost 15,000 people were killed in the natural disaster.

The flood in 1995 was the worst natural disaster in our country.

Niche product *[Adjective + Noun]* *(a product that appeals to a small and specialized group of people.)*

As a manufacturer of a niche product, we are at an advantage.

You should identify a niche product that you want to sell.

Nutritional deficiency *[Adjective + Noun]* *(a lack of essential nutrients such as vitamins and minerals.)*

Diseases of the nervous system are mainly caused by nutritional deficiencies.

Vitamin supplements and minerals can make up for nutritional deficiencies.

Nutritious food *[Adjective + Noun]* *(food that contains substances which help your body to stay healthy or to grow properly.)*

Milk, beans, apples and oranges are very healthy and nutritious food.

If you want to stay healthy, you should do lots of exercises and eat nutritious food.

Nuclear family *[Adjective + Noun] (a family unit that consists only of a mother, a father, and their children.)*

He was born and grew up in a nuclear family.

She has been living in a nuclear family.

Nourishing meals *[Adjective + Noun] (meals that make you strong and healthy.)*

She prepares nourishing meals for her daughter daily.

It is very important to feed our children nourishing meals so they could study well and promote their health.

Natural disaster *[Adjective + Noun] (a natural event such as an earthquake, cyclone, tornado, etc. that causes great harm, damage or loss of life.)*

The earthquake which occurred in 1990 was considered one of the greatest natural disasters in our history.

The government should encourage people to help the victims of natural disasters.

COLLOCATIONS/O

Occupational accident [Adjective + Noun] (an injury to an employee that happens in the workplace.)

He was the victim of the occupational accident last month.

Occupational accidents account for more than 90% of occupational disabilities.

Online shopping [Noun + Noun] (the activity of purchasing products or services over the Internet.)

One of the advantages of online shopping is selection.

An increasing number of consumers are finding online shopping quite convenient to make purchases.

Outdoor life [Adjective + Noun] (life existing or happening outside.)

Tom likes the outdoor life with his cousins.

The outdoor life provides him a sense of completeness.

Obey an order [Verb + Noun] (to do what someone orders or asks you to do.)

Their children are taught to obey orders.

If you fail to obey orders, you will be disciplined.

With careful training, her dog has learned to obey several orders.

Occupational hazard [Adjective + Noun] (a danger that people doing a particular job may suffer or experience.)

An occupational hazard that nightclub workers may face is hearing loss.

Occupational hazards that typists are likely to suffer from are hand injuries.

Odd number [Adjective + Noun] (any whole number that is not able to be exactly divided by two, such as 1, 3, 5, 7, etc.)

The numbers 1, 3, and 5 are odd numbers, but 2 and 4 are even numbers.

Offer a job *[Verb + Noun] (to give someone a job if they want it.)*

We decided to offer him the job.

It will be incredibly exciting if I am offered a job.

Offer an explanation = provide an explanation *[Verb + Noun] (to give a reason and explain why something was done or happened.)*

Peter offered a detailed explanation for his decision to close the company.

Bill hasn't been offered a satisfactory explanation as to why he was fired from his job.

Offer condolences *[Verb + Noun] (to show sympathy and sadness to the family or close friends of someone who's just died.)*

We offered our condolences to Kim and her family on their tragic accident.

They offered their sincere condolences to the victims' families.

Offer your services *[Verb + Noun] (to offer your time skills, ability, or knowledge to help someone or an organization.)*

John sometimes offered his services as a lawyer for free.

You can get paid online by offering your services as a freelance writer.

Office hours *[Noun + Noun] (the number of hours during the day when people work in an office.)*

If you have any requirements, please call me during our office hours from 9:00 to 5:00.

I'm not often free during office hours.

Our service is only available during office hours.

Office job *[Noun + Noun] (a job based in an office that people work at desks with computers, phones, etc.)*

Tom felt bored with his nine-to-five office job.

Her mom would like her to have an office job.

Old age *[Adjective + Noun]* *(the time of someone's life when they are old.)*

My parents have saved enough for their old age.

My teacher doesn't like to travel much because of old age.

Only just *[Adverb + Adverb]* *(a very short time ago; by a small amount or degree.)*

I'm still full. I've only just had dinner!

They've only just left.

Helen's got only just enough time to finish the essay.

I've got only just enough money to buy the house.

Open an account *[Verb + Noun]* *(to start having a bank account.)*

Jack opened his first bank account when he went to university.

A majority of young people open bank accounts these days.

Open an investigation *[Verb + Noun]* *(to begin an investigation into a case (as by the police).*

The police will open an investigation into the crash of flight 702.

The police have opened an investigation into the accident.

Opening hours *[Adjective + Noun]* *(the time during which a business, such as a bar, restaurant, shop, or bank is open for business.)*

The bar's opening hours are from 9.30 am to 11.30 pm.

The fashion shop will extend its opening hours until later in the evenings.

Organic farming *[Adjective + Noun]* *(farming without using artificial fertilizers or pesticides.)*

These days, organic farming has become a popular trend all over the world.

An increasing number of people tend to buy fresh fruits and vegetables which are produced from those implementing organic farming practices.

Owe an apology [Verb + Noun] *(to think or feel that you should apologize to someone.)*

I think I owe you an apology for what I did to you.

I think you owe her an apology for what you said.

Outward journey [Adjective + Noun] *(a journey in which you are going away from home/ leaving for a particular destination.)*

John got lost on the outward journey.

The date of our outward journey is 14th June.

Open fields [Adjective + Noun] *(fields uninterrupted by woods or houses.)*

The open fields make the place so attractive.

Sometimes we like to wander around the open fields.

One of the perks of the job [Noun + Noun] *(a payment or benefit that you get from your job in addition to your wages, such as money, meals, a mobile phone, a car, etc.)*

One of the perks of the job is that you get free theater tickets.

I always get discounts on flights, it's one of the perks of the job.

Office block [Noun + Noun] *(a large multistorey building that contains many offices of more than one company.)*

There are many high-rise office blocks in the city center.

I used to work in the office block next to the mall.

Out of print [Phrase] *(a book that is no longer available to buy because it is no longer being published.)*

His book, which used to be a best seller, is now out of print.

Although the book is now out of print, but you can easily borrow it from libraries.

Organic food [Adjective + Noun] *(food that is produced by not using artificial chemicals and methods.)*

Sarah says that she only eats organic food since it is healthy and nutritious.

People are willing to pay for organic food although it is more expensive.

Oval face [Adjective + Noun] *(face that is shaped like an egg.)*

Rosie has a beautiful oval face.

She is tall and has curly dark hair and an oval face.

Over-priced restaurant/hotel [Adjective + Noun] *(restaurant/hotel that is too expensive (worth less than the price that is being charged))*

They threw his birthday party at an overpriced restaurant.

We had a boring and expensive dinner at an overpriced hotel restaurant.

It's always too expensive to buy drinks at an overpriced hotel.

Old friend [Adjective + Noun] *(someone who has been your friend for a long time.)*

My old friend, Paul, will come to visit me tomorrow.

Peter and Joe are old friends. They've known each other since they were in college.

Obey the law [Verb + Noun] *(to do what a law says that you must do.)*

You ought to obey the law.

Not a lot of drivers are obeying the new traffic laws.

COLLOCATIONS/P

Play a part (in something) *[Verb + Noun]* *(to perform a particular role, or to be involved in something.)*

Alcohol plays a part in 60 percent of traffic accidents.

Our thanks to everyone who has played a part in building the school for disable children.

Stress plays a part in the development of illnesses like heart disease and cancer.

Platonic relationship *[Adjective + Noun]* *(a relationship that is friendly but does not involve sex.)*

He wants to keep a platonic relationship with her.

Tom and Mary have a platonic relationship because he and she are not ready for a dating relationship at present.

Put into practice *[Verb + Noun]* *(to carry out in action/ to use something in actual situations.)*

His idea is good, but it's hard to put into practice.

He suggested me put his advice into practice immediately.

She plans to put these new ideas into practice as soon as he can.

Play an integral part in something *[Phrase]* *(to play a part that is necessary for something to be complete)*

Electricity plays an integral part in our daily lives.

Insurance plays an integral part in crisis management.

Play a big/important part in something *[Phrase]* *(to play an essential part of something.)*

Luck plays a big part in making people rich

Water plays an important part in everyday life

Play the guitar *[Verb + Noun] (to play a musical instrument, usually made of wood, with six strings and a long neck, played with the fingers or a plectrum.)*

Does your father play the guitar?

Tom plays guitar in a band.

Powerful engine *[Adjective + Noun] (an engine that has great power or force.)*

His car has a very powerful engine.

That is a fast blue car with a very powerful engine.

Pitch dark *[Adverb + Adjective] (completely dark, extremely dark.)*

It was pitch dark when he left the house yesterday.

Look! The sky is becoming pitch dark!

It was a pitch dark and very chilly night.

Pose a problem *[Verb + Noun] (to cause a problem.)*

Her ill health poses serious problems for her future.

The high rate of inflation poses serious problems for the government.

Pack a suitcase *[Verb + Noun] (to put someone's clothes and other possessions into a suitcase.)*

His wife was still packing her suitcase when the taxi came.

My brother hasn't packed his suitcase yet.

Painful memory *[Adjective + Noun] (a memory that makes you feel upset, ashamed, or unhappy.)*

The photographs about the war brought back many painful memories.

John has lots of painful memories from his past.

Painfully slow *[Adverb + Adjective] (extremely slow.)*

His recovery after a very serious accident has been painfully slow.

Solving water pollution is a painfully slow process.

Painfully shy *[Adverb + Adjective] (extremely shy.)*

Sarah is painfully shy, so it's hard for her to make new friends.

I was painfully shy when I was a teenager. I didn't want to meet people who I didn't know.

Pair work *[Noun + Noun] (a type of learning activity, such as a language that is done by two students working together.)*

Pair work plays an important role in ESL classes.

You should do some pair work to practice new expressions right after learning them.

Part company *[Verb + Noun] (to end a relationship (cease to be together) such as a marriage, friendship, etc.)*

Tom and Mary parted company last year.

Richard and Joe have parted company for over 2 years.

Pass (the) time *[Verb + Noun] (to do something to prevent yourself from becoming bored.)*

I played games to pass the time when I was on a long flight.

Tom read a book to pass the time when he was on the bus.

Pass a test *[Verb + Noun] (to be successful in a test or an examination by achieving the required standard in such an exam, a test, etc.)*

Jennifer has passed her driving test.

Tom would have passed the test easily if he had studied hard.

Pay a bill *[Verb + Noun] (to pay the total amount of money written on a bill.)*

Bob always pays his bills on time.

My mom always pays the telephone and electricity bill at the end of every month.

Pay increase = pay rise *[Noun + Noun] (an increase in someone's wage or salary.)*

All the workers of the factory have been awarded a 2% pay increase/ pay rise.

The directors of his company awarded themselves five percent pay rises.

We all agreed that bill deserved a pay rise.

Peace and quiet *[Noun + Noun] (a calm quiet situation in which someone is not annoyed by noise or disturbance.)*

I would like to have a little peace and quiet at the moment.

I'm doing yoga. Can I have a little peace and quiet, please?

Personal belongings *[Adjective + Noun] (personal possessions that you own.)*

Mark packed his personal belongings in a bag and left.

Please check your personal belongings before you leave the hotel.

Phone rings = telephone rings *[Noun + Verb] (if your phone rings, it makes a loud clear sound.)*

You might be in trouble if your phone rings in private places.

Her phone rang while she was taking a shower in the bathroom.

Pick (one's) nose *[Verb + Noun] (to remove dried mucus from inside someone's nose with their finger.)*

Stop picking your nose, peter!

It would be disgusting if you picked your nose in front of lots of people.

Piece of advice *[Noun + Noun] (a particular suggestion that someone gives you* *about the best thing to do in a particular situation.)*

Would you like me to give you a piece of advice?

I think you should get a piece of advice from your doctor.

Piece of equipment *[Noun + Noun] (a tool, machine, or another particular item that you need for a particular job or activity.)*

A camera is the most important piece of equipment you need to buy at the moment.

I think the air conditioner is a useful piece of equipment for my bedroom.

Piece of information *[Noun + Noun] (a particular fact or detail about somebody/something.)*

Paul gave me a very interesting piece of information.

John read an interesting piece of information in the local newspaper this morning.

Piece of music *[Noun + Noun] (a pattern of sounds made by musical instruments, voices, etc. that is pleasant or exciting to listen to.)*

They rehearsed a new piece of music for the concert.

It was a beautiful piece of music.

Piece of paper *[Noun + Noun] (one sheet or scrap of paper that you use for writing and drawing on.)*

Lucy handed him a piece of paper with an email address written on it.

Peter wrote Jane's number on a piece of paper, but then he lost it.

Place an order *[Verb + Noun] (to order something/ to submit an order for a product/ to make a request to buy something.)*

His secretary placed an order for a new computer yesterday.

We could place our order by telephone or on the internet.

Point of view *[Noun + Noun]* *(a particular perspective or way of judging a situation based on a particular aspect.)*

From a scientific point of view, the invention is extremely important.

From my point of view, the house is too small.

Play a part *[Verb + Noun]* *(to perform a particular role in a particular situation or activity, especially in a way that is important.)*

I personally want to thank all my friends and members of my family who have played a part in my success.

According to the survey, drunk driving plays a part in the car accidents.

Poor eyesight *[Adjective + Noun]* *(bad eyesight)*

His eyesight was so poor. He couldn't see everything on the screen clearly.

Mark suffered from poor eyesight and might no longer read books or news properly.

Popular belief = widespread belief *[Adjective + Noun]* *(an idea or something that most people believe is true or real.)*

There is popular belief that he has been resigned.

Contrary to popular belief, you don't need a lot of money to be happy.

There is widespread belief that cocaine is an addictive drug.

Pose a risk (to someone) *[Verb + Noun]* *(to be a risk; to create a risk of danger or harm to someone.)*

Smoking poses a health risk for both smokers and non-smokers.

Air pollution, water pollution, and noise pollution pose serious risks to the environment.

Pretty good *[Adverb + Adjective]* *(quite good/ very good.)*

Tom did a pretty good job being an actor.

Your new dress looks pretty good.

John looks pretty good in his new suit.

Pretty well *[Adverb + Adverb] (fairly well)*

Bill is pretty well fed up with doing the same things at the same time every day.

Joe speaks English and Japanese pretty well.

Private life *[Adjective + Noun] (aspects of someone's life such as relationships, interests, and activities as distinct from their public life.)*

I'm not concerned about his personal life.

His personal life is not my concern.

Public opinion *[Adjective + Noun] (the opinions or attitude that the majority of people in a society have about a particular matter.)*

The social media has a powerful impact on public opinion.

The prime minister has failed to change public opinion on the issue of law and order.

Put on weight *[Verb + Noun] (to gain weight/ to get fat.)*

I think you are putting on a little weight. You had better go on a diet.

Jane put on weight because she drank too many soft drinks.

Put out something *[Verb + Noun] (to stop something from burning or shining.)*

To put out a candle/light/fire

Please put out your cigarette.

Put up prices *[Verb + Noun] (to increase prices of something.)*

They haven't put up prices of their products for over two years.

We put up prices when inflation increased.

Put up your hand *[Verb + Noun] (to raise your arm if you want to say something.)*

Jane usually puts up her hand in the class.

Mark put up his hand when the teacher called his name.

Pay a compliment *[Verb + Noun] (to say something nice to someone; to praise someone for something.)*

Jane complained that her husband never paid her any compliments anymore.

John paid Lucy a compliment when he told her she was smart.

He wanted to pay her a compliment so he told her he liked her beautiful eyes.

Pay your respects (to someone) *[Verb + Noun] (to visit someone, or to send them a greeting or a message of good wishes as a sign of respect for them.)*

Tom and Mary went to pay their respects to their grandparents.

Please pay my respects to your parents.

Pay your last respects (to someone) *[Verb + Noun] (to show respect or affection towards a dead person by attending his/her funeral.)*

David and hid friends came to pay their last respects to Mr. Thompson.

Nearly 300 people attended the funeral to pay their last respects to a very popular gentleman.

Pay tribute to someone *[Verb + Noun] (to say or do something that shows your respect or admiration to someone.)*

Many of mark's friends gathered to pay tribute to him.

They gathered to pay tribute to a great man.

Pouring with rain *[Verb + Noun] (to rain heavily/ to rain very hard.)*

Although it was pouring with rain, he still went for a walk.

It was pouring with rain, so I had no choice but to stay inside.

Package holiday *[Noun + Noun] (a holiday arranged by a travel agent for which you pay a fixed price that includes the cost of the accommodation, transport, and sometimes entertainment.)*

Thousands of people go on a package holiday every week.

It's always cheaper to go on a package holiday.

Is there anything else you would like to know about your package holiday?

Picturesque village *[Adjective + Noun] (a village which is very pretty or charming.)*

His family lives in a very picturesque village in japan.

There is a picturesque village in that mountain.

Passport control *[Noun + Noun] (the area in an airport where your passport is checked.)*

Tom was stopped when he went through passport control

It may take you ages to get through passport control at the airport.

Pop the question *[Verb + Noun] (to ask somebody to marry you/ to propose marriage.)*

Mark is going to pop the question to his dream woman.

I remember he popped the question while we were having dinner at this Japanese restaurant.

Personal best *[Adjective + Noun] (the best achievement or result someone has ever had so far in a sporting event.)*

Helen was swimming faster than usual because she wanted to beat her personal best.

Jack set a personal best in the race of 6 minutes 30 seconds.

His personal best in the race was a six-minute mile.

Personal trainer *[Adjective + Noun]* (someone whose job is to give you advice and guidance on how to exercise effectively.)

My brother is working as a personal trainer.

Jessica has hired a personal trainer and works out with him every day.

Play truant *[Verb + Noun]* (to miss or stay away from classes without permission.)

His parents didn't know that he had played truant regularly.

He used to play truant and usually wrote his own absence notes.

Private school *[Adjective + Noun]* (a school that receives financial support from private individuals or a private organization rather than from a government or public agency.)

Sarah teaches English at a private school.

His parents have decided to send him to a private school.

Public school *[Adjective + Noun]* ((in the US) a school that receives financial support from the government and is controlled by the government.)

Bill attended a public school.

Mary sent her daughter to a public school in Boston.

Prescription charges *[Noun + Noun]* (the amount of money the patient pays for medicines prescribed by a doctor.)

Some people who live in poverty may be exempt from prescription charges.

Did you have to pay the prescription charges?

Pull a muscle *[Verb + Noun]* (to injure a muscle due to moving too quickly or stretching it too far.)

His doctor said he has pulled a muscle in his back.

You might pull a muscle if you don't do stretches before running or swimming.

Page-turner [Noun + Noun] *(a book that is so exciting or interesting that you would like to read it quickly.)*

Her book is a real page-turner with various interesting plots.

His latest novel is a wonderful page-turner.

Permanent address [Adjective + Noun] *(a fixed address.)*

Could you please give me your permanent address?

My permanent address has not changed in the past 7 years.

Property market [Noun + Noun] *(the buying and selling of land and houses.)*

My father is knowledgeable about the commercial property market.

Peter has a comprehensive knowledge of the residential property market.

Put down a deposit [Verb + Noun] *(to pay an amount of money as a guarantee that you agree to pay the rest later when you buy something expensive such as a car or a house.)*

They've just put down a deposit on a new house in town.

He managed to accumulate sufficient funds to put down a deposit on a car.

Pavement café = sidewalk café [Noun + Noun] *(a part of a coffeehouse or café which is outdoors or on the pavement where vehicles do not normally go.)*

Let's have a drink on a pavement café.

We are sitting at an outside table in a pavement café near the shopping mall.

Places of interest [Noun + Noun] *(places that are interesting.)*

There are many places of interest in Liverpool.

We visited a lot of places of interest on our vacation in Beijing.

Public spaces [Noun + Noun] *(social spaces that are generally open and accessible to the public.)*

A park is a public space with a slide, swing set and swimming pool.

Smoking is banned in public spaces and workplaces.

Public transport *[Noun + Noun] (a system of buses, subways, trains, etc. Running on fixed routes that everyone can use.)*

I prefer to use public transport rather than use my own car.

He had to rely on public transport to travel to school.

There is no public transport in this area.

Piece of music *[Noun + Noun] (a pattern of sounds made by musical instruments, voices, etc. that is pleasant or exciting to listen to.)*

They rehearsed a new piece of music for the concert.

It was a beautiful piece of music.

Play by ear *[Phrase] (to play a piece of music without looking at the musical notes.)*

He can play Chopin's music by ear.

Peter can play anything on the piano by ear.

Pour down *[Phrase] (to rain very hard.)*

It started to pour down after dinner.

I was walking in the park when it started to pour down heavily.

Pay in cash *[Phrase] (to pay for something using money in the form of notes and coins.)*

You'll get a discount if you pay in cash.

We had to pay in cash for the tickets.

Pay the full price *[Verb + Noun] (to pay the full amount of money for something.)*

He had to pay the full price because he paid by credit card.

Children under five don't have to pay the full price for the ticket.

Paperback book [Noun + Noun] *(a book that has thick paper covers.)*

She spent the morning yesterday reading a paperback book

He was sitting at the desk, reading a paperback book with a cigar in his mouth.

Public library [Adjective + Noun] *(a nonprofit library often supported with public funds, intended for public use.)*

Sarah works as a librarian in a public library.

There is a public library in my place from which I can borrow books.

Put someone in jail [Verb + Noun] *(to put someone in a prison/ imprison.)*

She was put in jail for 2 years.

He was put in jail for his drug use.

Pursue a hobby [Verb + Noun] *(to be involved in an activity that you enjoy doing.)*

She was too busy studying to pursue a hobby.

He was determined to pursue a hobby of career in programming.

Physical well-being [Adjective + Noun] *(the state of being physically healthy.)*

Physical well-being has a great influence on our mental health.

Do you want to examine your physical well-being?

Peaceful countryside = tranquil countryside [Adjective + Noun] *(the area outside towns and cities which is quiet and calm (without noise, excitement, etc.))*

My parents love to live in a peaceful countryside.

My uncle's house is located in a peaceful countryside.

They live in an ancient cottage, in a perfectly tranquil countryside.

Pace of life *[Noun + Noun] (the speed of life at which changes and events occur.)*

He likes the rapid pace of life in the city.

They moved to a countryside, seeking a slower pace of life.

Pose a threat *[Verb + Noun] (to be a threat/ to create the threat of danger or harm to someone.)*

Drunken drivers pose a serious threat to other people on the streets.

Drugs, robbery, and burglary pose a major threat to the society.

People skill *[Noun + Noun] (the ability to effectively communicate, understand and empathize.)*

Coaching is a critical people skill.

Patience is a valuable people skill in every profession.

Package tour = package holiday *[Noun + Noun] (a holiday at a fixed price organized by a travel agent, with arrangements for transportation, accommodations, meals, tour guides, etc.)*

A package tour to Italy can really save you a great deal of money.

We bought a package tour around Europe and stayed in a five-star hotel by the sea.

Probationary period *[Adjective + Noun] (a period of time that employees are exempt from certain contractual items and they are allowed to terminate the employment for any reason.)*

He was 3 months into his probationary period before having a contract of employment.

His employer extended his probationary period because the contract allowed them to do this.

Pocket money *[Noun + Noun] (money that parents give to their kids regularly/ a small amount of money someone spends for minor expenses.)*

I give my son $10 a week pocket money.

She saved her pocket money to buy her mother a scarf

He's already spent all his pocket money for this month.

He plans to look for a part-time job to earn a little pocket money.

Play a joke/trick on someone [Verb + Noun] *(to do funny things to someone that makes them look silly or feel embarrassed.)*

Tom is always playing jokes on his siblings.

The kids played a joke on their father.

He played a cruel trick on his friend.

Pointed face [Adjective + Noun] *(a face with a point at the end.)*

Her boyfriend has a pointed face and big blue eyes.

His girlfriend has a pointed face with a small nose, and short black hair.

Provide for your family [Verb + Noun] *(to make enough money to support your family.)*

I need to get to work and provide for my family.

My uncle worked really hard to provide for his family.

Promising career [Adjective + Noun] *(a career that is likely to be successful.)*

David gave up a promising career in medicine to become a priest.

Her father gave up a promising career in law to fight for his country.

Take the minutes [Verb + Noun] *(keep the official record of a meeting.)*

Who is going to take the minutes of the meeting?

Jane was designated to take the minutes of the meeting.

Pay/face a heavy fine [Verb + Noun] *(to pay a lot of money as a punishment for* *not obeying a rule or law.)*

He had to pay a heavy fine for speeding.

If found guilty, he faces 2 years in jail and a heavy fine.

Pass up the opportunity/chance *[Verb + Noun] (if you pass up an opportunity or a chance, you do not take advantage of it.)*

I won't pass up the opportunity to go to Harvard University.

When tom's friend gave him the chance to share the apartment, he couldn't pass up the opportunity.

Put off (making) a decision *[Verb + Noun] (to delay making a decision.)*

He wants to put off making the decision a while longer.

If you don't have sufficient information, you should put off making the decision.

Sometimes we need to put off making the decision even though we have deadlines.

COLLOCATIONS/Q

Quaint old building [Adjective + Noun] *(a building that has an old-fashioned attractiveness or charm.)*

It was a quaint old building.

We climbed to the roof of the quaint old building.

Quick learner = Fast learner [Adjective + Noun] *(someone who learns things quickly.)*

He is a quick/fast learner, and his English gets better day by day.

Mary is a quick learner, but Tom is a quicker learner.

Quality of life [Noun + Noun] *(the level of satisfaction and comfort in someone's life.)*

My quality of life improved significantly once I finished paying for my MBA education.

Our quality of life has improved dramatically since we moved to the countryside.

Quick fix [Adjective + Noun] *(a solution to a problem that can be done or implemented quickly although it may not last long.)*

A new tax will be enacted as a quick fix.

We are still looking for quick fixes to these problems.

Quick reply [Adjective + Noun] *(a rapid response to a letter or email.)*

Thank you for your quick reply to my email.

Wait me a minute. I would like to send a quick reply to an email first.

Quietly confident [Adverb + Adjective] *(feeling confident, but not talking proudly about it.)*

Richard felt quietly confident after the interview.

Jessica looked quietly confident before her driving test.

Quit a job *[Verb + Noun] (to leave a job permanently.)*

Bill quit his job after 6 months working for a bank.

Peter didn't understand why his wife quit her job.

Quit drinking *[Verb + Noun] (to stop drinking alcohol.)*

Quit drinking or you will die soon.

Her father has quit drinking for over 5 months.

Quit smoking *[Verb + Noun] (to stop smoking cigarettes.)*

Although it's difficult to quit smoking, I think you can do it.

We'll find the right methods to help you quit smoking.

Quite a lot/a bit *[Adverb + Adverb] (quite a large number or amount.)*

With 50 dollars, you could buy quite a lot of candies and chocolates.

I have been spending quite a lot on clothes recently.

Quite agree *[Adverb + Verb] (to agree completely.)*

I quite agree with your point of view.

We don't quite agree with his viewpoint. He's not absolutely right.

Quite good *[Adverb + Adjective] (fairly good.)*

The food and drinks in this restaurant are various and quite good.

The movie was quite good, but the game was much better.

Quite often *[Adverb + Adverb] (fairly often.)*

We used to go fishing quite often, but now we rarely go.

I see them quite often because they are my neighbors.

Quite right *[Adverb + Adjective] (completely right (to show that you strongly agree with someone))*

What my teacher said was quite right.

His English speaking skill is improving, but some of his pronunciation isn't quite right yet.

Quite sure *[Adverb + Adjective] (completely sure or absolutely sure.)*

Are you quite sure you will attend my party tonight?

I'm not quite sure.

I am not quite sure where he is.

Quick snack *[Adjective + Noun] (a small amount of food that is eaten between regular meals.)*

When Sarah came home from school, she always eats a quick snack before doing her homework.

Let's stop for a quick snack.

COLLOCATIONS/R

Round face [Adjective + Noun] (a face that is shaped like a circle or a ball.)

His girlfriend has a lovely round face.

I saw a beautiful girl with a round face this morning.

Reach a decision [Verb + Noun] (to make a decision.)

Have you reached the decision yet?

I have to reach a decision tomorrow.

It took him four days to reach a decision.

Renewable energy [Adjective + Noun] (energy that is collected from renewable resources, which are naturally, such as solar, wind, tidal, wave, and hydroelectric power, etc.)

Solar, wind and water can be used to create renewable energy.

It is true that renewable energy sources are not sufficient enough to meet the world's energy requirements.

Rustic charm [Adjective + Noun] (a charm that is simple, old-fashioned and typical of the countryside.)

I love the rustic charm of the simple and old cottage.

He bought an old rocking chair since he loved its rustic charm.

Regular customer [Adjective + Noun] (someone who buys goods or services from a shop or company frequently.)

She is one of our regular customers.

His business quickly built up a network of regular customers.

React against something [Phrase] (to show dislike or opposition in response to what someone wants you to do because you do not like their rules or ideas.)

She reacted against learning everything she had been taught.

Raise capital *[Verb + Noun] (to get a large amount of to start a business or to finance its activities.)*

He is trying to raise capital for his startup online.

As an entrepreneur, he must be excellent at raising capital to finance his business.

Racial discrimination *[Adjective + Noun] (unfair treatment of a person or a group because they are members of another race.)*

The elimination of racial discrimination should be implemented as soon as possible.

A group of five people are claiming race discrimination against their former employer.

Rain hard *[Verb + Adverb] (rain heavily.)*

I will take the raincoat with me in case it may rain hard this evening.

It was raining hard, so we had to stay inside.

Raise doubts *[Verb + Adverb] (to make someone unsure or have doubts (about something))*

The tragic accident has raised doubts about the safety of the car.

Her death has raised about the safety of the sleeping pills.

Raise (someone's) hopes *[Verb + Noun] (to make somebody hope or expect something very much.)*

It would be unfair to raise your hopes at this early stage.

Don't raise her hopes until you know for sure the results.

Raise questions *[Verb + Noun] (to bring issues or questions that need to be discussed and dealt with to somebody's attention.)*

We raised questions about pay rises for employees at the meeting.

Recent accidents are bound to raise questions about the safety of vehicles on the streets.

Raise taxes *[Verb + Noun] (to make people pay a tax with a higher rate.)*

The government is going to raise taxes on wealthy people.

According to experts, the new president would increase taxes for approximately six million families.

Raise your voice *[Verb + Noun] (to speak loudly and clear, especially when you are angry.)*

The teacher had to raise his voice when his students didn't hear what he said.

Please try not to raise your voice. My little daughter is sleeping.

I had never heard my father raise his voice like that before.

Rapid growth *[Adjective + Noun] (a rapid rise/ development.)*

There has been a rapid growth of population in china recently.

Canada has recently witnessed a rapid economic growth.

Rate of return *[Noun + Noun] (a proportion of the money that was originally invested and returned as profit.)*

We are very happy since the average rate of return on all our investments has remained above 7%.

The actual rate of return of the project is estimated to significantly increase to 20%.

Rave review *[Adjective + Noun] (a very enthusiastic review of a book, movie/ film, etc.)*

Brian Tracy's books have received rave reviews from the readers.

His performance in the film has received rave reviews from the audiences.

Reach an agreement *[Verb + Noun] (to come to an agreement after discussing or* *negotiating something with someone.)*

After two days of negotiation on the terms of the service fees, we reached an agreement and signed a contract.

They haven't reached an agreement with the unions on the pay rises yet.

Read aloud = read out loud *[Verb + Adverb] (using the voice to say words loud enough for other people to hear.)*

Please read the essay aloud so everyone can hear it

Jane read the letter aloud to her family members.

Real life *[Adjective + Noun] (what happens in the real world rather than in a story, film, or in your imagination.)*

In the movie, John plays a bad guy, but in real life, he's kind and gentle.

Tom is not interested in science fiction very much. He prefers stories about real life.

Reasonable explanation *[Adjective + Noun] (an explanation that is reasonable, most people can accept or believe that it is true or correct.)*

He came up with a reasonable explanation for his absence.

There was no reasonable explanation for what happened.

Reasonably priced *[Adverb + Adjective] (available at a fair price (not too expensive))*

We bought a reasonably priced house.

Food and drinks in that restaurant are reasonably priced.

Return a call *[Verb + Noun] (to telephone somebody back after not answering their call.)*

My mother left me a message to return her call.

She is still waiting for me to return her call.

Return flight *[Noun + Noun] (a flight going back)*

How much is a return flight to New York?

There's a return flight to Hong Kong in 2 hours.

Return home *[Verb + Noun] (to go back home or come back home.)*

My son returned home after midnight.

When did you return home from the trip?

Return ticket *[Noun + Noun] (a ticket for travel to a place, and then back again.)*

If you buy a return ticket, it will be cheaper than two one-way tickets.

Bill was not allowed to board the flight back to Canada due to his invalid return ticket.

Right away *[Adverb + Adverb] (immediately)*

My cousin called and asked me to come over right away.

Sorry, I have to go now. My boss wants to see me right away.

Right now *[Adverb + Adverb] (at this moment; immediately.)*

My boss isn't available in the office right now, but he'll be back soon.

I'm feeling very happy right now.

Mom says you have to call her back right now!

Room for improvement *[Noun + Noun] (the action of improving something or making something better.)*

Your pronunciation is better but there is some room for improvement.

There's still room for improvement in your essay.

Root cause *[Noun + Noun] (the main or fundamental cause for the occurrence of a problem.)*

It is widely argued that poverty is the root cause of crime.

Is materialism the root cause of crime?

Root crop *[Noun + Noun] (a plant such as carrots, potatoes, ginger, etc. That its roots can be used for food.)*

Many people eat root crops such as carrots, potatoes, ginger to prevent illnesses.

This soil is perfect for the growth of root crops.

Rough draft *[Adjective + Noun] (the first version of a piece of writing, a book or a document which is unedited.)*

Peter has just completed a rough draft of his first book.

The teacher requested him to edit or rewrite the rough draft of his essay.

Rough estimate *[Adjective + Noun] (an approximate estimate (not exact estimate))*

Could you please give me a rough estimate of the cost of making your house safe?

The figure I'm about to give you is just a rough estimate.

Rough idea *[Adjective + Noun] (a vague or general idea, concept; an estimate.)*

Since he couldn't remember the exact date, so he just gave a rough idea of when they had left.

Most students have a rough idea of what is meant by consciousness.

Round number *[Adjective + Noun] (any number that ends in 0, such as 10, 20, or 2250.)*

Let's just estimate the cost in round numbers.

I want a round number on tax return.

Run the risk of *[Verb + Noun] (to do something unpleasant that may result in a bad result.)*

I don't want to run the risk of hurting my girlfriend's feeling, so I won't tell her the truth.

People who smoke a lot of cigarettes run the risk of suffering from lung cancer.

Running late *[Verb + Adverb] (to do things or arrive in places later than the time that is planned or expected.)*

Let's hurry up, or we're running late.

The bus was running late, so I didn't arrive in my office on time.

Running low *[Verb + Adjective] (something has been almost used up (there is not much of it left))*

We're running low on beer, so I'd better go and get some more.

My car is running low on gas, so I'd better fill up it with gas.

Rain heavily *[Verb + Adverb] (to rain a lot/ rain hard.)*

It was raining heavily during the night.

The football match was postponed when it started to rain heavily.

Return journey *[Adjective + Noun] (the journey back from a place or destination.)*

My return journey took longer because the flight was delayed.

On my return journey, I stopped to see the beautiful beach.

Runny nose *[Adjective + Noun] (if you have a runny nose, your nose produces more mucus and liquid than usual, usually because of a cold, allergy, or crying.)*

She's got a runny nose.

My son had a bad cough and a runny nose.

Read something from cover to cover *[Verb + Noun] (to read a book, newspaper or magazine all the way through from the first page to the last page.)*

She read that novel from cover to cover in less than eight hours.

On the bus, he read the newspaper from cover to cover.

I am planning to read this book from cover to cover in one day.

Rented accommodation [Adjective + Noun] *(property such as a house, flat, or hotel room that is used by a person who pays rent to the owner.)*

They are staying in rented accommodation at the moment.

We lived in rented accommodation for the first two years of university.

Run a business [Verb + Noun] *(to be in charge of a business such as a company, a shop or a store.)*

It's quite challenging to run a business nowadays.

My brother started to run a coffee business since he left the university.

Residential area [Adjective + Noun] *(an area where has only private houses, not offices and factories.)*

This area now becomes a residential area with many new houses.

Her planned accommodation is in a residential area and within 2 kilometers of the school and the child health clinic.

Run-down building [Adjective + Noun] *(a building that is in very bad condition.)*

The city has been restoring a run-down building.

This is a photo of the run-down building where the thief was hiding.

Rained off [Phrase] *(if a sport or other outside activity is rained off, it is canceled or postponed due to heavy rain.)*

The football match was rained off.

The cricket match has been rained off again.

Relaxed atmosphere [Adjective + Noun] *(a situation or place that is comfortable and informal.)*

It's a very friendly restaurant with a relaxed atmosphere.

The hotel had a nice relaxed atmosphere.

There has been a more relaxed atmosphere at the party since he left.

Rosy cheeks [Adjective + Noun] (cheeks that are pink and pleasant in appearance.)

His daughter has beautiful rosy cheeks.

Her rosy cheeks always make her look so healthy.

Rush hour [Noun + Noun] (the time of day when traffic is at its heaviest.)

Many accidents happened during the rush hour this morning.

I always try to avoid travelling during the rush hour.

Razor-sharp mind [Adjective + Noun] (if you have a razor-sharp mind, you are able to think very clearly and quickly.)

My brother's got a razor-sharp mind.

One of his great gifts is a razor-sharp mind.

Reveal your true character ≠ conceal/ hide your true character [Verb + Noun] (to show your true character.)

He's revealed his true character as a liar.

She revealed her true character to tom when he disagreed with her.

Jane is able to hide/conceal her true character and feelings.

Respectable family [Adjective + Noun] (a family that is worthy of respect.)

Mary comes from a very respectable family.

Tom was adopted into a respectable family.

Raise children = bring up children [Verb + Noun] (to look after a child until he or she is an adult.)

The married couple brought up six children.

Jane raised her children in just the same way her parents did.

Ruin someone's career [Verb + Noun] *(to end someone's career.)*

That sex scandal ruined her career.

Alcohol and drugs ruined his career and caused his death.

Rewarding job [Adjective + Noun] *(a job that gives you a lot of personal satisfaction.)*

Being a bus driver is a rewarding job.

Teaching kids about money is a challenge and a rewarding job.

Reach a verdict [Verb + Noun] *(to decide whether someone is guilty or not after having heard the facts given at a trial.)*

The jury took six hours to reach a verdict of guilty.

After seven hours of deliberation, the jury finally reached a verdict of not guilty.

Run into difficulty = get into difficulty [Verb + Noun] *(find yourself in a difficult situation.)*

He soon ran into difficulty with debt.

Four people were rescued from a car that had run into difficulties.

We have got into difficulties with the new project.

Run into trouble/problems/difficulty [Verb + Noun] *(to start to have trouble/ problems/difficulty.)*

His business ran into financial difficulties.

They ran into trouble with the law.

He quickly ran into problems when he set up his camera.

He immediately ran into trouble when he was accused of having a sexual relationship with his female employee by abusing his position.

Rustle up a meal *[Verb + Noun] (to make or prepare a meal very quickly.)*

My mom can rustle up a meal in 20 minutes.

She was trying to rustle up a meal before the guests arrived.

COLLOCATIONS/S

Seek a job [Verb + Noun] *(to look for a job)*

She is seeking a job as a secondary school English teacher.

Tom quit his job last month. He is seeking a new job now.

Shake off a cold [Verb + Noun] *(get rid of a cold.)*

She is trying to shake off a cold.

He had not been able to shake off a cold and had lost a lot of weight.

Social network [Adjective + Noun] *(a network of friends, colleagues, and other personal relationships.)*

He is disabled and doesn't have much of a social network.

She has a wide social network of supportive friends and colleagues.

Slippery customer [Adjective + Noun] *(a clever and deceitful customer.)*

He is a seriously slippery customer so be careful what you say to him.

Don't believe what she says. She is a slippery customer.

Sense of adventure [Noun + Noun] *(willingness to try new things or take risks.)*

The young man has an immense sense of adventure.

Jack has a great sense of adventure and likes to keep his spirits high.

Sign up for a course [Verb + Noun] *(to enroll on a course.)*

You'll get a discount if you sign up for a course on network theory and analysis today.

I've already signed up for a course on artificial intelligence taught by Professor Matthew Jackson of Stanford University.

Satisfy the demands of *[Verb + Noun] (to meet the demands of.)*

Sometimes we do not satisfy the demands of our customers.

They are managing to satisfy the demands of their customers at present.

Stimulate growth *[Verb + Noun] (to encourage something to grow or develop.)*

Innovation has stimulated the growth of economy.

An increase in the amount of CO_2 has stimulated the growth of tropical trees.

Surrounding countryside *[Adverb + Verb] (the land and scenery of a rural area.)*

From the top of the hill, we had a clear view of the surrounding countryside.

Our luxury hotel is well situated for exploring the surrounding countryside.

Soft skills *[Adjective + Noun] (personal qualities that enable people to communicate well with each other and work well together.)*

They are focusing on soft skills such as communications and team building.

Stream of visitors *[Noun + Noun] (a continuous flow of people.)*

A stream of visitors was coming out of the church.

A steady stream of visitors came to visit the museum.

Substantial meal *[Adjective + Noun] (a big meal.)*

We had a substantial meal last night.

We are enjoying a substantial meal for dinner.

Strictly forbidden *[Adverb + Verb] (not allowed in a strict way according to a law, or rule.)*

Smoking is strictly forbidden in the office.

The use of mobile phones is strictly forbidden in the library.

Submit a tender [Verb + Noun] (to present a formal offer to supply goods or do work at a stated price.)

Our company is going to submit a tender for the construction contract.

Ensure that you must correctly sign all appropriate tender forms before submitting a tender.

Start up a business [Verb + Noun] (to bring a business into existence.)

Smith left the company last year to start up his own business.

He decided to start up a business with a capital of $5,000.

Strongly oppose [Adverb + Verb] (to disagree strongly with somebody's plan, policy, etc. Often by speaking or fighting against it.)

They strongly opposed changing the law.

Many local residents are strongly opposed to the tax reform.

Strongly influence [Adverb + Verb] (to have a strong effect on the way that someone behaves or thinks.)

Most young smokers are strongly influenced by their friends.

What factors strongly influenced your decision to study overseas?

Strongly recommend [Adverb + Verb] (to strongly advise someone that they should do something because it is good or useful.)

The doctor strongly recommended that he should get more exercise.

It is strongly recommended that all machines in the factory should be checked every month.

Strongly support [Adverb + Verb] (to support or believe in somebody or something very much.)

Tom's family strongly supported his decision of studying overseas.

A large percentage of people in the city strongly support the plans to build a new hospital.

Strongly condemn *[Adverb + Verb]* (to criticize something or someone strongly; to express very strong disapproval of someone or something, usually for moral reasons.)

They strongly condemn the attack against their allies.

Many women strongly condemn gender violence in Africa.

Strongly feel = feel strongly *[Adverb + Verb]* (to have a very strong, or passionate opinion about something or attitude towards something.)

This is something Julie feels strongly about.

Mark felt (that) he had to apologize.

Strongly argue *[Adverb + Verb]* (to speak angrily to someone because you totally disagree with them.)

Their children are always strongly arguing.

Her brothers are always arguing.

Strongly object *[Adverb + Verb]* (to strongly express opposition to or dislike of something or someone.)

The majority of people in the town strongly object to the building of the new factory.

They strongly object to being charged for parking.

Safe and sound *[Adjective + Adjective]* (free from damage, danger, hurt or injury.)

It was a rough trip, but we arrived home safe and sound.

We are glad to see you here safe and sound.

Sales figures *[Noun + Noun]* (the number of sales of products sold within a particular time frame.)

The year's sales figures improved significantly.

Sales figures improved considerably during the promotion campaign.

Sales force [Noun + Noun] *(all the employees of a company whose job is to sell products or services.)*

With so many new products, our company needs to have a strong sales force.

The sales force of my father's company is large and strong.

Satisfy a need [Verb + Noun] *(to give or provide what you need or want.)*

Your products must satisfy the needs of your customers.

The online course is designed to satisfy the needs of college students.

Satisfy a requirement [Verb + Noun] *(to fulfill what a requirement states or specifies.)*

Cheryl has satisfied all the requirements for the job in a foreign company.

Richard was unable to satisfy the requirements to teach in a foreign country.

Save lives [Verb + Noun] *(to stop or prevent someone from dying or being killed.)*

We might save lives if we become blood donors.

His doctors are working hard to find new medical treatment to save his life.

Sense of direction [Noun + Noun] *(a person's natural ability to know which direction you're going in, even when you are in an unfamiliar place.)*

They were wandering through the forest without a sense of direction.

Jack didn't get lost thanks to his good sense of direction.

Serious accident [Adjective + Noun] *(an accident which is dangerous enough to badly injure or kill someone.)*

Did you see the serious accident between a car and a motorbike last night?

The traffic was congested due to a serious accident.

Serious illness *[Adjective + Noun] (a very bad illness/ a dangerous illness.)*

Sally was really sad when the doctor said that her father had a serious illness.

His grandfather was diagnosed with a serious illness.

Serious injury *[Adjective + Noun] (a very bad injury which requires someone to have an immediate treatment in a hospital.)*

A majority of serious injuries we treat are caused by road traffic crashes.

Luckily, there were no serious injuries in the car accident.

Serious mistake *[Adjective + Noun] (a very bad mistake which causes a lot of problems.)*

Tom made a serious mistake when deciding to study abroad.

It was a serious mistake when I decided to quit my job.

Seriously damage *[Adverb + Verb] (badly damage something so that it is broken, or spoiled.)*

His career was seriously damaged by the scandal.

Her house was severely damaged by fire last night.

Set a date *[Verb + Noun] (to decide a particular date on which something will take place or happen.)*

We haven't set a date for the next meeting yet.

They have set the date for their wedding.

Set a goal *[Verb + Noun] (to identify something that you would like to achieve or accomplish over a particular period.)*

John set his goal to earn $50,000 by the end of the year, and he accomplished it.

Sally's goal was to buy a house by the end of 2013, and she achieved it.

Set a standard [Verb + Noun] *(to identify a certain level of quality that you would like to achieve.)*

Jessica sets herself high standards.

Peter James set the standard for writing his next book.

Set a table = lay a table [Verb + Noun] *(to place forks, knives, spoons, plates, glasses, napkins, etc., on the table before a meal is served.)*

Julie, could you please set the table?

She was making the salad while I was setting the table.

Set an alarm [Verb + Noun] *(to set the time at which a device will ring or make a loud sound.)*

Bill set his alarm clock for 6.00 a.m.

My son's got to be at school by seven, so he set his alarm for 5:30 a.m.

Set fire to = set on fire [Verb + Noun] *(to deliberately cause something to start burning.)*

The insane man accidentally set himself on fire.

Her car was set on fire when she was away.

The thieves set fire to the bank.

Set free [Verb + Adjective] *(to grant freedom to someone or something.)*

Peter set the dog free from his kennel.

After catching the fish, he set them free.

Set menu [Adjective + Noun] *(a complete meal in a restaurant or café with a limited number of courses for a fixed price.)*

Would you like to order a set menu?

This set menu has an inclusive price of £25 comprising a main course and drink.

Short memory *[Adjective + Noun] (if you have a short memory, you forget things quickly.)*

He has a short memory, so he might forget what you asked him to do.

Social life *[Adjective + Noun] (the part of a person's time spent with friends and social activities.)*

My father's got a very busy social life.

I have to work seven days a week, so I don't have much of a social life.

Solve a crime *[Adjective + Noun] (to find out who committed a crime.)*

It took the police nearly 10 years to solve the crime.

Sherlock Holmes is very talented at solving crimes.

Solve a problem *[Verb + Noun] (to find the way or solution to deal with a problem or a difficulty.)*

We are making attempts to solve the problem of radioactive waste.

The government should take measures to solve the problems of air pollution and water pollution.

Spare time *[Adjective + Noun] (leisure time/ free time (time when you are not working))*

Tom spends a lot of his spare time playing games.

I usually read books on business in my spare time.

Spend time *[Verb + Noun] (to use time doing something or being somewhere.)*

I spend a lot of time at my office almost every day.

I think you need to spend more time studying English.

Stand trial *[Verb + Noun] (to be put on trial or to be judged for a crime in a court of law.)*

The young men were due to stand trial for robbery.

He'll be standing trial for perjury and obstruction of justice next month.

Stay awake *[Verb + Adjective] (to remain awake.)*

Last night, I drank coffee late, so I couldn't sleep and stayed awake all night.

We stayed awake, talked and watched films all night.

Stay put *[Verb + Verb] (to stay in the same place or position/ to not move or go anywhere.)*

I've decided to stay put and not to move to New York.

Stay put. I'll go and get some drinks. I'll be back in a minute.

Stay tuned *[Verb + Verb] (to keep listening to a radio broadcast or to keep watching a television show.)*

Let's stay tuned for these announcements.

Let's stay tuned for the latest news, and then we can watch something else.

Steady job *[Adjective + Noun] (a job that offers a constant and reliable income (you will be paid regularly).*

It isn't easy to find a steady job these days.

Her parents would like her to get a steady job

Steady relationship *[Adjective + Noun] (a serious relationship that continues for a long period of time.)*

We have been in a steady relationship for nearly 3 years so far.

How long were you in a steady relationship before you got married?

Still (be) alive *[Adverb + Adjective] (living and not dead yet.)*

That plant is still alive although it looks dead.

I couldn't believe that he was still alive for a week without any food.

Straight after *[Adverb + Adverb] (right after/ immediately after.)*

I'm going to school straight after breakfast.

You shouldn't have a bath straight after a big meal.

Straight ahead *[Adverb + Adverb] (straight forward/ in front of someone.)*

Instead of driving straight ahead, you turn left at the next intersection.

Don't turn left. Keep walking straight ahead towards the river.

Straight answer *[Adjective + Noun] (an honest and true answer.)*

Could you please give me a straight answer?

He was unable to give a straight answer in the consultation meeting today.

Straight away *[Adverb + Adverb] (immediately (without any delay))*

I need someone to help me straight away. It's an emergency.

I'm feeling ill, so I should go and see a doctor straight away.

Strictly speaking *[Adverb + Verb] (in actual fact (used for showing that something is completely accurate))*

Strictly speaking, they are not in a good relationship.

Strictly speaking, the book is not a novel. It is a short story.

Strike a balance (between something and something) *[Verb + Noun] (to find a balanced position in order to satisfy some of the demands of both sides.)*

A balance must be struck between quality and productivity.

I need to strike a balance between my work life and my family life.

Sure sign *[Adjective + Noun] (a piece of evidence that something is happening or certainly true.)*

He ignored what I said, which was a sure sign that he disliked me.

An increasing number of people who are unemployed is a sure sign of problems in the economy.

Stream of traffic [Noun + Noun] *(a long and continuous moving line of vehicles in the traffic.)*

There was a constant stream of traffic behind us in the rush hour.

There was an endless stream of traffic on the highway this morning.

Sunny smile [Adjective + Noun] *(a bright, friendly and pleasant smile.)*

Lucy captivates everyone with her sunny smile.

Jane's sunny smile warmed my heart.

She is a young woman with a very sunny smile.

Shower of rain [Noun + Noun] *(a short period of rain.)*

I got caught in a shower of rain while going for a walk.

There was a heavy shower of rain last night.

Safe journey [Adjective + Noun] *(a journey or a trip when someone is safe (said to someone when they are about to leave for a long journey or trip))*

I wish you a safe journey.

Mom rang to wish me a safe journey.

Scheduled flight [Adjective + Noun] *(a regular flight organized by the company that owns the plane.)*

I will wake up early tomorrow morning since I'll have a scheduled flight to Los Angeles.

The scheduled flight was delayed due to bad weather.

Smooth flight [Adjective + Noun] *(a comfortable trip in an airplane which does not shake or frighten you.)*

We had a very smooth flight from Sydney.

I wish you have a smooth flight.

Sandy beach *[Adjective + Noun] (a beach which is covered with sand.)*

My children are playing on the sandy beach.

We looked for sea shells and walked along the sandy beach.

Secluded beach *[Adjective + Noun] (a beach which is peaceful, and not visited by many people.)*

His family is living on a secluded beach.

A local man gave us directions to a very beautiful and secluded beach.

Stunning landscape *[Adjective + Noun] (a landscape which is very impressive or beautiful.)*

The stunning landscape of chrome hill filled me with energy and a sense of freedom.

A great way to help us get away from pressure in our daily lives is to enjoy the stunning landscape and spectacular views.

See eye to eye *[Phrase] (to agree or have the same opinion with someone about something.)*

Jane and her mother don't see eye to eye on many things.

Peter and his girlfriend see eye to eye on most things, so they don't often have fights.

Strike up a relationship *[Verb + Noun] (to begin a relationship with someone.)*

Cheryl struck up a relationship with a doctor soon after she arrived in New York.

Peter tried to strike up a relationship with a young woman he had helped.

Send an attachment *[Verb + Noun] (send an email with other documents to provide extra information.)*

It is highly recommended to send an attachment in pdf format.

When you send an attachment, always remember to tell the recipient what it is.

Surf the web [Verb + Noun] *(to look at various websites on the internet.)*

John spends a lot of time every day just surfing the web.

We may be tracked by websites when we surf the web.

Season ticket [Noun + Noun] *(a ticket for a certain activity, or series of events that can be used several times within a particular period of time and costs less than paying separately for each use.)*

I hold a season ticket for all our team's games.

My season ticket expires on May 15th.

Set a record [Verb + Noun] *(to achieve the best results in a particular activity, especially sport, or sales.)*

Adam has set a record in the marathon.

Our team set a record for online sales next year.

Sports centre [Noun + Noun] *(a building where people can go to play various sports.)*

There's a tennis court in the sports centre near my house.

A new sports centre has just been opened in this area.

Yesterday I played tennis with him at the sports centre.

Sports facilities [Noun + Noun] *(buildings, services, and equipment that are provided for doing sports.)*

Our town has excellent swimming pools and sports facilities.

I wish there were more sports facilities in our area.

Slap up meal [Adjective + Noun] *(a large and very good meal.)*

My parents went for a slap-up meal on their wedding anniversary.

He's planning to treat her to a slap-up meal at a really good restaurant.

Spoil your appetite *[Verb + Noun] (to eat something that makes you no longer be hungry or want to eat less at the next meal.)*

Don't eat too many nuts before dinner or you'll spoil your appetite.

You'll spoil your appetite for lunch if you eat too much fruit now.

Single-sex school *[Adjective + Noun] (a school that admits students of one sex only (either males or females, but not both))*

My daughter attended a single-sex school for 4 years.

Do you like to go to a single-sex school?

Sit an exam *[Adjective + Noun] (to take an exam/ do an exam.)*

All students have to sit an exam at the end of the school year.

I'm going to sit an exam tomorrow morning, so I need to go to bed early tonight.

Sick leave *[Adjective + Noun] (a period of time during which an employee is allowed to be absent from work because of illness.)*

She's been on sick leave since last week.

He broke his leg, and he was on sick leave for three weeks.

Speedy recovery *[Adjective + Noun] (a quick recovery from an illness or injury.)*

We hope you have a speedy recovery/ we wish you a speedy recovery.

I wish him a speedy recovery.

Sore throat *[Adjective + Noun] (a painful condition of the throat someone feels when swallowing or talking, typically caused by inflammation due to a cold or other viruses.)*

Fever and sore throat are the initial symptoms of the disease.

Lemon and honey are homespun remedies to soothe sore throats.

Single room *[Adjective + Noun] (a room with a single bed for one person to stay in.)*

I had booked a single room for him.

I would like a single room with a TV, a shower, and a balcony, please.

A single room at the Austin hotel costs $70 a night.

Spacious room *[Adjective + Noun] (a large room which has a lot of space inside it.)*

He led us to a spacious room, full of paintings.

It was a spacious room painted in yellow.

I think all of the guests will be able to fit into the spacious living room.

Smart clothes *[Adjective + Noun] (formal clothes/ neat and attractive clothes.)*

Most people wear smart clothes to a job interview.

Peter usually wears smart clothes to work, like a jacket and tie.

Sense of humour *[Noun + Noun] (an ability to express humour, find things amusing and give someone the chance to say funny things.)*

Sarah's boyfriend has a great sense of humour.

Tom made us laugh a lot at the party last night. He has a really good sense of humour.

Sales figures *[Noun + Noun] (a number of sales of particular products or services within a particular period.)*

The company had monthly sales figures of half a thousand units.

The sales figures for august and September were £14,123.

The store's sales figures are always high.

Set up a business *[Verb + Noun] (to formally start a business or establish a new company.)*

I plan to set up my own business.

You'll have to work longer hours when you set up a business.

Stiff competition *[Adjective + Noun] (strong competition/ tough competition.)*

Graduates face stiff competition in getting jobs.

Small grocery stores face very stiff competition from the large supermarket chains.

Slender figure *[Adjective + Noun] (a figure that is tall and thin in an attractive or graceful way.)*

She has a beautifully slender figure.

The young lady has a tall and slender figure.

Slim figure *[Adjective + Noun] (a figure that is attractively thin.)*

The young girl has a lovely slim figure.

His girlfriend has a very slim figure.

Shopping centre *[Noun + Noun] (an area containing a lot of different shops.)*

We are planning to go shopping at the new shopping centre tonight.

The new shopping centre that was constructed last year is close to my house.

Shopping mall *[Noun + Noun] (a large building containing various retail stores; usually includes restaurants and a convenient parking area.)*

I went to a shopping mall near the hotel where I was staying to buy a new sweater.

Would you like to go to the shopping mall with me tonight?

Sing along *[Phrase] (to join in singing with someone who is singing or while a record, radio, or musical instrument is playing.)*

She enjoys singing along to the radio.

My sisters and I sometimes sing along.

Sunny spell [Adjective + Noun] *(a short period of time during which sunny weather lasts.)*

The weather forecast is for dry, sunny spells.

It is forecast to rain at first, with sunny spells later.

Shop around [Phrase] *(to visit different shops to compare the price and quality of the same or a similar item before buying)*

He is shopping around for a new computer.

When my mom's buying a flight, she always shops around to make sure she gets the best deals.

Shop assistant [Noun + Noun] *(a person whose job is to serve customers in a shop.)*

The shop assistant was friendly and helpful.

Alice works as a shop assistant in a computer store.

Slash prices [Verb + Noun] *(to reduce prices by a large amount.)*

They slashed the prices of their smartphones by 60%.

We are planning to slash prices to increase our sales next month.

Sales page [Noun + Noun] *(a page specifically used to promote a product or service.)*

If people read my sales page, they'll certainly know what I'm selling.

Your sales page should include the eye-catching elements that can turn visitors into paying customers.

Show adverts [Verb + Noun] *(to display adverts on TV.)*

We never show adverts with religious or political content.

We only want to show adverts we believe our customers want to see.

Social media [Adjective + Noun] *(websites and computer programs that enable users to communicate, share information or to participate in social networking.)*

We use social media to promote our business.

The company uses social media to market its products.

Serve a prison sentence [Verb + Noun] *(to be in jail.)*

You'll have to serve a prison sentence if you commit a crime.

He had to serve a prison sentence for illicit sex with a minor.

Suffer from a disease [Verb + Noun] *(to have a particular illness.)*

No one would like to suffer from a disease.

Has he suffered from a heart attack or stroke?

Sexually-transmitted disease [Adjective + Noun] *(infections that are passed from one person to another through having sex, especially vaginal intercourse, anal sex and oral sex.)*

HIV is a sexually transmitted disease.

Her husband has an incurable sexually transmitted disease.

Snow-covered mountain [Adjective + Noun] *(a mountain that is covered or topped with fallen snow.)*

We saw the snow-covered mountain at dawn.

The snow-covered mountain peaks glistened at sunrise.

Sun-drenched ground/garden [Adjective + Noun] *(a ground or garden that receives a great deal of sunshine.)*

We were sipping coffee in the sun-drenched garden.

She likes to sit on a sun-drenched ground with the palms of.

Spectacular view [Adjective + Noun] *(a view which is very dramatic or extremely impressive.)*

From the third level of the tower, visitors enjoyed a spectacular view of Paris.

We had a spectacular view of New York harbor from our room.

Secluded beach [Adjective + Noun] (a beach that is not seen or visited by many people.)

Alice told me she wanted to live on a secluded beach.

We found a secluded beach where we spent the day and saw the dolphins playing in the waves.

Square face [Adjective + Noun] (a face that is very equal in regards to width and length.)

Her boyfriend has a square face.

His girlfriend has a lovely square face and beautiful hair.

Shoulder-length hair [Adjective + Noun] (hair that is long enough to reach your shoulders.)

She has light brown shoulder length hair.

The woman with shoulder-length hair is a lawyer.

Striking appearance [Adjective + Noun] (an unusual and interesting appearance that attracts attention.)

Peter has a striking appearance and gets along well with all his friends.

Jane was known for her striking appearance and graceful manner.

Self-confident manner [Adjective + Noun] (behaviour that is considered to be confident in yourself and your abilities.)

Tom has a self-confident manner and a striking appearance.

Jack impressed the audience with his self-confident manner.

Smiling face [Adjective + Noun] (a facial expression of pleasure or amusement.)

I was impressed by her smiling face.

He loves to see your smiling face.

Smooth skin [Adjective + Noun] (skin that is completely even with no roughness.)

The baby has lovely smooth skin.

Cucumber juice is excellent for a beautiful smooth skin.

Swarthy skin [Adjective + Noun] (a natural dark skin.)

He has dark eyes, short black curly hair, and swarthy skin.

That was a woman with a simple hair style and swarthy skin.

Sparkling eyes [Adjective + Noun] (eyes that shine brightly.)

Tom caught Sarah's hands and looked into her sparkling eyes.

Her shiny smile and sparkling eyes happily agreed.

Slender girl [Adjective + Noun] (a girl who is tall and thin in an attractive or elegant way.)

I saw a slender girl of about 18 standing at the front door this morning.

She is a tall slender girl who won the beauty contest last year.

Salt and pepper hair [Noun + Noun] (hair that has a mix together blend of black and gray hair, usually men.)

My father's salt and pepper hair has now turned completely white.

He is a tall man with salt-and-pepper hair and big brown eyes.

Street children [Noun + Noun] (homeless children who live and survive on the streets of a city or town.)

They have been trying to help street children in their area.

In order to survive, many street children have to beg or steal or sell their bodies in prostitution.

Slow-moving traffic [Adjective + Noun] (the very slow movement of vehicles along a road or street.)

We got caught in queues of slow-moving traffic.

He got frustrated by slow-moving traffic.

Social skills = communication skills *[Adjective + Noun]* *(skills that people use to successfully communicate and interact with each other.)*

She enjoys playing games that require social skills.

Having good social skills will provide you more chances to be successful in business.

Skilled workers = skilled professionals *[Adjective + Noun]* *(workers who have acquired special skills, training, and knowledge in their work.)*

Demand for skilled workers is always high.

The average skilled workers earn over $15,000 per year.

Train drivers and pilots are highly skilled professionals.

Set high standards *[Verb + Noun]* *(to establish very good standards.)*

Tom always sets high standards for himself.

If teachers want to set high standards for their students, they need to do the same for themselves.

Swallow your pride *[Verb + Noun]* *(to forget your pride and accept something that makes you feel embarrassed or ashamed.)*

She finally had to swallow her pride and asked for a second chance.

Jane swallowed her pride and called her son to apologize.

He had to swallow his pride and admit that he was wrong.

Start a family *[Verb + Noun]* *(to begin having children.)*

It's time for us to start a family.

Tom and Mary want to get married and start a family soon.

Single parent *[Adjective + Noun] (a parent who brings up their children alone, without a partner.)*

It's difficult for a single parent to work full-time.

If you are a single parent, it'll be hard for you to bring up a child on your own.

Set up home *[Verb + Noun] (if you set up home, you start an independent life in your own flat or house.)*

They got married, and set up home in Roma.

Tom decided to leave the US and set up home in France.

Strike up a friendship *[Verb + Noun] (to start a friendship with someone.)*

She would like to strike up a friendship with me.

He has managed to strike up a friendship with a beautiful girl.

Spoil a friendship *[Verb + Noun] (to make a friendship become worse.)*

Our friendship was spoilt after a fierce argument.

Peter has spoiled his friendship with Sarah.

Special friend *[Adjective + Noun] (someone whom you want them to be more than your friend, but has not yet been elevated to "girlfriend" or "boyfriend" status.)*

Mary and peter are special friends.

I thought Lucy was his special friend.

Studio flat = studio apartment *[Noun + Noun] (an apartment containing one main room with a very small kitchen, and a bathroom, usually designed for one or two people.)*

Peter lives in a nice studio flat in London.

Tom and his wife live in a studio flat with no bedroom.

Second home *[Noun + Noun] (a house that someone owns but lives in only for short periods/ a place where you spend a great deal of time but do not live in permanently.)

We have a second home on the lake.

His office is his second home.

Severely punished [Adverb + Verb] (to be punished in a very strict way.)

The murderer will be severely punished.

If anyone breaks the law, they will be severely punished.

Suffer the consequences [Verb + Noun] (to be punished for what someone has done.)

The accused decided to tell the truth and suffer the consequences.

If you break the law, you will have to suffer the consequences.

Strike up a conversation [Verb + Noun] (to start a conversation with someone in an informal way.)

Tom struck up an interesting conversation with a beautiful girl at the pool yesterday.

Alice struck up an interesting conversation with a young man on the bus this morning.

Settle a dispute [Adjective + Noun] (to put an end to an argument or a disagreement.)

Our top priority is to settle the dispute as soon as possible.

We want to settle the dispute peacefully.

Strongly advise [Adverb + Verb] (to give your opinion to someone that they should do something in a particular situation because it is good or useful.)

Her mother strongly advises her to lose weight.

My friend strongly advised me to sell my old car.

Sentimental value [Adjective + Noun] (the value of an object in terms of its *sentimental associations rather than material worth.)*

She keeps these pictures because they have sentimental value for her.

He doesn't want to get rid of his old bike because it has sentimental value.

Say a word *[Verb + Noun]* *(to tell someone about something.)*

Don't say a word about the accident to her mom.

If you say a word of this to my parents, I'll be really upset.

I promise not to say a word to her about it.

Strictly speaking *[Phrase]* *(being completely accurate.)*

Strictly speaking, they are not a married couple.

Strictly speaking, you are not qualified for the job.

Strictly speaking, Tom and Mary have been living apart for years.

COLLOCATIONS/T

Take a stroll [Verb + Noun] *(to take a leisurely walk/ to go for a leisurely walk.)*

We took a stroll through the city last night.

Would you like to take a stroll down to the market with me?

Tough question [Adjective + Noun] *(a question that is difficult to answer.)*

That was a really tough question to answer.

His teacher called on him with a tough question, and he didn't know the answer.

Take issue with [Verb + Noun] *(to disagree or argue with someone about something.)*

Bill took issue with Mary about the cost of the house.

I take issue with parents who physically punish their children in a strict way.

Tom wants to take issue with the last statement Dr. James made.

Target market [Noun + Noun] *(a particular group of customers at which a business has decided to aim its marketing efforts and ultimately its products towards.)*

Young women are their target market for skin care products.

Our target market is consumers who are aged between 20 and 40.

Take the view [Verb + Noun] *(to believe or to have an opinion (about something))*

She takes the view that the economy will improve next year.

A large percentage of people take the view that children should not be physically punished.

Take on responsibility [Verb + Noun] *(to assume new responsibility for something.)*

My sister takes on responsibility for childcare.

He doesn't want to take on responsibility for this program.

I could take on responsibility for things I'm not responsible for.

Talk nonsense *[Phrase]* *(to say something that is unreasonable or stupid.)*

Please stop talking nonsense about politics!

He was talking nonsense in the meeting.

Tell a secret *[Verb + Noun]* *(to disclose or reveal a secret.)*

It can be easy for children to tell a secret rather than keep it.

He didn't know how to tell the secret without hurting his girlfriend.

Tell someone's fortune *[Verb + Noun]* *(to say or anticipate what will happen to someone in the future.)*

The old woman told his fortune with the cards.

He laid the cards out and told her fortune.

To pursue higher education *[Verb + Noun]* *(to follow an education and training at a college or university where subjects are studied at an advanced level.)*

His parents encourage him to pursue higher education.

Many women have decided to pursue higher education and careers instead of getting married and giving birth to children.

To progress rapidly in their career *[Verb + Adverb]* *(to develop quickly in someone's career.)*

Peter progressed rapidly in his career as a lawyer.

Students who choose to seek a job straight after high school instead of pursuing higher education are likely to progress rapidly in their career.

To obtain a lot of real experience *[Verb + Noun]* *(to get a lot of real experience.)*

I hope I will have a chance to obtain a lot of real experience for my chosen profession.

This job may offer you a good opportunity to obtain a lot of real experience.

Take a gap year *[Verb + Noun]* *(to spend a year between leaving school and starting university on working and/or traveling.)*

Tom took a gap year to work right after graduating from high school.

My brother is planning to take a gap year and go backpacking in Canada.

The generation gap *[Noun + Noun]* *(the difference in attitude, experiences, opinions, habits, and behaviour between young and older people that causes a lack of understanding each other.)*

We are trying to bridge the generation gap with our children.

He feels that the generation gap he has with his father is doubly big.

Take up a profession *[Verb + Noun]* *(to start doing a job)*

He took up a profession in the medical field.

When she left university, she took up a profession as an accountant in a foreign company.

To relieve pain/ ease pain/ lessen pain/ alleviate pain *[Verb + Noun]* *(to make pain or another bad physical feeling less unpleasant.)*

Do you know how to relieve pain without medicine?

These are effective medications to ease pain.

He used marijuana to lessen/alleviate pain.

Take a holiday *[Verb + Noun]* *(to go and stay in another place and do things for pleasure on an occasion when you do not work or study.)*

My parents are planning to take a holiday in Canada this year.

Jane is going to take a holiday with her family in Ireland next month.

Take a trip = go on a trip *[Verb + Noun] (to go somewhere for pleasure, usually for a short time, and come back again.)*

Her whole family takes a trip to California.

They went on a trip to the mountains.

We took a trip down the river.

Take a liking to *[Verb + Noun] (to begin to like someone or something.)*

Jack took an immediate liking to rose.

Mark had taken a liking to Lucy on their first meeting.

Take (sb's) temperature *[Verb + Noun] (to measure the temperature of somebody's body by using a thermometer)*

The nurse took his temperature and said that he was ok.

The doctor took her temperature and found that she is running a fever.

The doctor examined my brother and took his temperature

Take a break = have a break *[Verb + Noun] (to have a short period of time to rest, eat, drink, go to toilet, etc. Before starting doing something again.)*

Let's take a short break about 15 minutes, then we return to the meeting at 1:30 pm.

Jane and her friends decided to take a break from college and do some travelling.

Take a risk *[Verb + Noun] (to do something that might be dangerous)*

If he was a good pilot, he wouldn't take a risk.

He took a big risk when he climbed the high mountain.

Take action *[Verb + Noun] (to do something to solve a particular problem or difficulty)*

We have to take action to deal with the problem before it's too late.

The government must take action immediately to stop the water pollution issue.

Take advice *[Verb + Noun] (to do what someone advises)*

He took his father's advice and left.

Tom took his doctor's advice and stopped drinking alcohol.

Take ages = spend ages *[Verb + Noun] (to take a long time)*

Peter usually takes ages to answer the phone.

She spent ages trying to print this document out.

Take care of *[Verb + Noun] (to care for or look after someone or something and provide the things that that person or thing needs.)*

Who's taking care of your dogs and kids while you're away?

She's old enough to take care of herself.

Take medicine *[Verb + Noun] (to swallow a tablet or drink a substance, especially a liquid in order to cure an illness)*

The doctor told him to take the medicine three times a day.

Please help me remind him to take medicine.

Take notes *[Verb + Noun] (to write down something when somebody is speaking, or when you are reading a book, etc.)*

John sat taking notes of everything his teacher said.

If you don't take notes what I'm saying, you may forget important details.

Take notice *[Verb + Noun] (to pay attention to something/ somebody)*

Don't take any notice of what he says.

Take no notice of what your father says – he's just in a bad mood.

Take part (in something) *[Verb + Noun] (to be involved in, or to participate in* an activity with other people)

All the kids took part in the Halloween games.

How many candidates took part in the interview?

Take place *[Verb + Noun] (to happen or occur, especially after previously being arranged or planned)*

The FIFA world cup takes place every four years.

She doesn't know exactly what took place in the restaurant.

Take time *[Verb + Noun] (to need a long time)*

It takes time to master a language, so be patient and don't give up too quickly.

It takes time to make changes in the education system.

Take turns (in something/to do something) *[Verb + Noun] (if people take turns to do something, they do it one after the other, or alternately to make sure it is done fairly)*

Her sister and she take turns cooking meals for the family, and today it's her turn.

We took turns driving the car.

Take your time *[Verb + Noun] (to spend as much time as you need in doing something, without hurrying)*

There's no time limit for this project, so you can take your time.

Don't be hurry, take your time to complete the assignments.

Tell a story *[Verb + Noun] (to share a story by reading it, recalling it, or making it up)*

Diana was telling a story to her children.

Susan tells her son bedtime stories every night.

Tight schedule *[adjective + noun] (many things to do in a short time)*

They are working to a tight schedule.

We have a very tight schedule today. We won't have enough time to hang out for beer as usual).

Time off *[noun + adverb] (time when someone is not at work or at school)*

Jane is going to take some time off to have a trip to Europe next week.

Jack needs some time off to pay his parents a visit.

Top floor *[adjective + noun] (the highest level of a building)*

We stay in a penthouse apartment on the top floor.

He loves to take photos from the top floor.

Try hard *[verb + adverb] (to put a lot of effort into doing something)*

Jane was trying hard not to laugh.

e has tried really hard but he can't convince her to come.

John tried really hard to win the game, but unfortunately, he lost.

Turn around *[verb + adverb] (to turn your body or head so that you're facing the opposite way)*

Jane turned around when she heard someone calling her name.

Take an interest in *[Verb + Noun] (to show you are interested in)*

Do your girlfriend's parents take an interest in you?

John takes an interest in politics these days.

Take a chance *[Verb + Noun] (to decide to do something even though it involves risk.)*

Lucy didn't know Jack but she took a chance on his honesty.

They took a chance on the weather and had the party outside.

Take advantage of *[Verb + Noun] (to make use of something well; to make use of an opportunity.)*

Mary took advantage of her son's absence to tidy his room.

Susan takes full advantage of his good nature.

Take (someone's) temperature *[Verb + Noun] (to measure someone's body temperature with a thermometer.)*

The nurse took my wife's temperature and said that she was running a fever.

She took my daughter's temperature and sent her to bed.

Take (sb) to court *[Verb + Noun] (to begin a legal case or to take legal action against someone.)*

Jane took her bad debtors to court.

The workers are threatening to take their employers to court for compensation.

You should take him to court if you can prove he is guilty.

Take a call *[Verb + Noun] (to answer an incoming telephone call.)*

"Someone is telephoning you, sir."

"Tell them I can't take their call at this moment."

If you take a call while you're at the meeting, you might get into trouble.

Take a look *[Verb + Noun] (to look at something with attention.)*

Take a careful look at this photo, and tell me who I am.

I asked the doctor to take a look at my throat and swollen glands.

Take a message *[Verb + Noun] (to write down or record a message from someone on the telephone and then give it to someone else.)*

He's not here now. Can I take a message for him?

Jane's not here at the moment. May I take a message for her?

Take a risk [Verb + Noun] *(to proceed in an action regardless of the possibility that something unpleasant or dangerous could happen.)*

Skydiving instructors usually take the most risks when working.

My wife and I took a big risk when we opened a western-style restaurant, but luckily everything went smoothly.

Take a seat [Verb + Noun] *(to sit down on something such as a chair, bench, sofa, etc.)*

Richard smiled at me when I took my seat on the opposite side of the table.

I walked into his room and he told me to take a seat.

Take a step [Verb + Noun] *(to put one leg in front of the other, as when walking or running; to perform a particular action in order to achieve a goal.)*

He quickly took a couple of steps towards the front door.

Take a step backward!

We are pleased that the government is taking steps to discourage age discrimination.

No wonder our boss has decided to take steps to cut down costs.

Take a test [Verb + Noun] *(to do a test.)*

I took my driving test last year.

My class is going to take a test tomorrow.

Take action [Verb + Noun] *(to do something to solve a particular problem or to achieve a goal.)*

We should urge the government to take action right away.

If the authorities don't take action immediately, all our forests will be destroyed.

Take someone's advice *[Verb + Noun] (to do what someone advises you to do in a particular situation.)*

She took her doctor's advice and stopped eating fast food.

Take my advice. Stop drinking alcohol and smoking cigarettes.

Take care *[Verb + Noun] (be careful; be alert.)*

Take care when you cross the street!

Take care when you drive home. The streets are slippery.

Take charge (of someone or something) *[Verb + Noun] (to take control or assume responsibility for someone or something.)*

When my wife and I went on vacation, my mother took charge of my son and daughter.

Jack will take charge of the company if his boss gets sick.

Take drugs *[Verb + Noun] (to use an illegal substance that affects someone physically or mentally.)*

I have never taken drugs in my life.

You will easily become addicted if you take hard drugs.

Take exercise = do exercise *[Verb + Noun] (to do physical activity to stay healthy and make your body stronger.)*

His doctor said he should take a lot more exercise and eat healthier food.

If you want to improve your heart and lung power, you should take exercise regularly.

Take someone hostage *[Verb + Noun] (to kidnap or seize and threaten to kill someone in order to get something.)*

A young woman was taken hostage by the gunmen.

His wife and daughter were taken hostage by the robbers.

Take long *[Verb + Adverb] (to take a large amount of time to do or finish something.)*

It won't take long to make a cup of coffee.

Luckily, the taxi didn't take so long, so I arrived at the office on time.

Take medicine *[Verb + Noun] (to swallow a tablet or drink a liquid to treat an illness.)*

The doctor said that he had to take the medicine three times a day.

Have you taken your medicine yet?

Take pride in *[Verb + Noun] (to be proud of someone or something you are closely connected with.)*

We take a great deal of pride in our sons and daughters.

Mark takes great pride in his appearance.

Take someone's place *[Verb + Noun] (to replace someone to do something.)*

No one could ever take his place in the team.

John resigned as a chairman in 2002 and Richard took his place.

Take someone/something seriously *[Verb + Adverb] (if you take someone or something seriously, you think that they are important and deserve your full attention.)*

I took what my teacher said so seriously.

Sarah takes her religious faith seriously.

Nobody takes her seriously because she herself is not serious at all.

Take up space *[Verb + Noun] (to fill or occupy an amount of space.)*

The table takes up too much space in the living room.

I think that the desk is taking up too much space in my room.

Tax cut *[Noun + Noun] (the act of reducing the rate of taxation.)*

Depending on the type of tax cut, jobs will be created in different ways.

We wish the government would introduce these tax cuts.

Tell someone the time *[Verb + Noun] (to tell somebody the time from a clock.)*

Billy is only four. He can't tell time yet. They are teaching the children to tell time at school.

I usually ask my son to tell me the time even though he is only four years old.

Excuse me! My watch doesn't work. Can you tell me the time, please?

Tell the difference *[Verb + Noun] (to recognize differences and be able to distinguish between similar people or things.)*

It's hard to tell the difference between the kittens.

I can't tell the difference between jack and Jill. They are identical.

It's really hard to tell the difference between their voices. They sound the same on the phone.

Top priority *[Adjective + Noun] (the most important thing that must be done first.)*

Safety must be given the top priority.

My top priority is to establish my career.

Top speed *[Adjective + Noun] (the maximum possible speed that something can travel at.)*

The car was running at top speed.

The top speed of my car is 60 miles per hour.

Travel light *[Verb + Adverb] (to travel without taking much luggage.)*

Since I prefer to travel light, so I only took a backpack on my trip to Florida.

My husband travelled light on his trip with nothing but a razor and few other personal items in his backpack.

Tell the truth [Verb + Noun] *(to say something in an open and honest way, without trying to hide anything.)*

To tell you the truth, I couldn't hear what you've just said. Could you repeat that, please?

I hope that john told us the truth.

Travel agent [Noun + Noun] *(a person or company whose job is to sell or arrange trips or tours for customers who want to travel.)*

My brother works as a travel agent.

Thanks to his travel agent, he was able to get a really cheap flight to Canada.

Travel arrangements [Noun + Noun] *(something that is done to prepare for a holiday or a journey, such as tickets, transportation, accommodations, tours, etc.)*

We have our travel agent handle all of our travel arrangements.

I'd like you to be in charge of all the travel arrangements.

Tiring journey [Adjective + Noun] *(a journey which makes you feel tired.)*

It was a long tiring journey on foot.

I'd never had such an extremely tiring journey before.

Take a picture = take a photo [Verb + Noun] *(to use a camera to produce a photograph.)*

May I take a picture of your house?

Do you want to take a picture of your family?

Tourist trap [Noun + Noun] *(a place, such as a restaurant, resort area, shop, or hotel that attracts and exploits many tourists by offering them overpriced goods and services.)*

That restaurant is just a tourist trap.

That market is a tourist trap which mostly sells expensive souvenirs.

Tie the knot *[Verb + Noun] (to get married.)*

Bill and Sarah will tie the knot next month.

After 3 years of dating each other, tom and Mary have finally decided to tie the knot next July.

Take up exercise *[Verb + Noun] (to learn or start doing exercise regularly as a habit.)*

Her mother always encourages her to take up exercise.

You are a bit overweight, so you should go on a diet and take up exercise.

Take a year out *[Verb + Noun] (if you take a year out, you spend a year working or travelling before going to university.)*

Many students choose to take a year out to travel before settling down to study for their bachelor's degree.

Instead of going straight on to the University of Law, he decided to take a year out to travel around the world.

Tuition fees *[Noun + Noun] (the amount of money that you have to pay for a course of study, especially at a college, university, or private school.)*

Tuition fees must be paid by the end of this month.

She had to borrow $15,000 a year to pay her tuition fees.

Take early retirement *[Verb + Noun] (if you take early retirement, you retire before the usual age for stopping working for a living.)*

My father decided to take early retirement at the age of 53.

I heard a rumour that the managing director is going to take early retirement.

Temporary work *[Adjective + Noun] (an employment situation where the employees* *take jobs for a limited time based on the needs of the employing organization.)*

He is looking for some temporary work to develop his new skills.

Our company has been offering temporary work to jobseekers.

The central character *[Adjective + Noun] (a person who plays the main role in a book, story, or film.)*

The central character in the story is the grandmother.

Tom Hanks is the central character in "a hologram for the king."

Take out a mortgage *[Verb + Noun] (to borrow a large amount of money from a bank in order to buy a house.)*

You can take out a mortgage if you want to buy a house.

In order to buy the house, he had to take out a mortgage.

Take after someone *[Verb + Noun] (to be like or look like an older member of your family in appearance or character.)*

Her son takes after her husband, both in appearance and character.

Don't you think our son takes after his father? No, he takes after his grandfather.

Take on employees *[Verb + Noun] (to start to employ people.)*

Our company is not taking on any new employees at the moment.

Is your company taking on any new staff at present?

Take out a loan *[Verb + Noun] (to borrow an amount of money, especially from a bank.)*

He's going to take out a loan to buy a car.

Alice took out a loan to pay for her apartment.

Tourist attraction *[Noun + Noun] (a place of interest where tourists visit for pleasure.)*

The church is the main tourist attraction of the city.

Paris is a popular tourist attraction.

Take up a musical instrument *[Noun + Noun] (to start learning a musical instrument.)*

Her parents encouraged her to take up a musical instrument.

Taking up a musical instrument is a great way to further develop your intellect and talents.

Thick fog *[Adjective + Noun] (a dense cloud of fog that makes very difficult to see through or breathe.)*

The flight has been delayed because of the thick fog.

He had to drive very carefully due to the thick fog.

The thick fog made it hard for us to see the road.

Tight budget *[Adjective + Noun] (a budget that severely limits the amount of money that can be spent; without much money to spend)*

They decorated their house on a tight budget

Tom lost his job. Now, he has a very tight budget.

Try something on *[Phrase] (to put on an item of clothing in order to see if it suits or fits you.)*

Could I try this shirt on, please?

She is looking forward to trying the dress on.

Toxic waste *[Adjective + Noun] (industrial or chemical waste materials that are harmful to living things and the environment.)*

The company was fined $6.5 million for dumping toxic waste into the river.

Toxic wastes were detected in the water samples.

Target audience *[Noun + Noun] (a particular group of people at which an* *advertisement, a product, a website or a television programme is aimed.)*

Teenagers are his target audience for the book.

Our target audience is consumers who are aged between 25 and 40.

The death penalty = capital punishment *[Noun + Noun] (a sentence or punishment of death, usually for a serious crime such as murder.)*

If convicted, he could face the capital punishment.

The murderer faced the death penalty for killing a victim of another race.

Tasty food *[Adjective + Noun] (food that has a very nice or pleasant flavor.)*

Our children like tasty food very much.

This restaurant has a plenty of tasty food.

Trial period = probation *[Noun + Noun] (period a period of time during which someone is tested to see whether they are suitable for work.)*

John has been hired for a trial period of 6 months.

She was asked to work for a trial period of 3 months.

Traditional medicine *[Adjective + Noun] (medical treatment using methods based on cultural beliefs and practices handed down from generation to generation.)*

She's tried traditional medicine.

Traditional medicine is used by a vast majority of people living in Asia.

Tree-lined walkway/street *[Adjective + Noun] (a walkway or street that has a row of trees on each side.)*

We were wandering down the gorgeous tree-lined walkway.

She lives in a large mansion on a tree-lined street.

Tanned face *[Adjective + Noun] (a face that has a brown skin colour because you have been in the sun.)*

The farmer has a tough tanned face and clear eyes.

He has a tanned face with some freckles.

Traffic congestion *[Noun + Noun] (heavy traffic/ traffic jam.)*

He arrived at the office late due to traffic congestion.

Traffic congestion is one of the biggest problems in our city.

Traffic congestion causes many disadvantages in the modern life.

Travel sickness *[Noun + Noun] (an unpleasant feeling in your stomach caused by the motion of a car, airplane, boat, etc.)*

She is suffered from travel sickness.

These medicines will help you to prevent travel sickness.

Tour guide *[Noun + Noun] (a person whose job is to show tourists around a place of interest and explain its history, architecture etc.)*

The tour guide explained the museum's history.

Our tour guide was really entertaining and knowledgeable.

Throw a sickie *[Verb + Noun] (if you throw a sickie, you pretend to be sick to take a day off work.)*

He threw a sickie to get Friday off.

She just didn't feel like going to work so she threw a sickie and went shopping.

When was the last time you threw a sickie?

Take a joke *[Verb + Noun] (to be able to accept or laugh at a joke that is about yourself.)*

If you want to play a trick, you must prepare to take a joke.

Tom has a great sense of humor, so he can take a joke.

The trouble with her is that she can't take a joke.

Throw a tantrum [Verb + Noun] *(to suddenly become very angry and unreasonable, often screaming, crying, etc.)*

Her son threw a tantrum and screamed loudly.

Alex threw a tantrum in the shop because her mom wouldn't buy her any sweets.

True friend [Adjective + Noun] *(a friend who knows you better than yourself, who you care for, and who cares for you.)*

He has become a true friend of mine.

A true friend would help you whenever you are in need.

Throw money at something [Verb + Noun] *(to try to solve a problem by spending spend a lot of money on it.)*

They threw money at the housing problem, but it had nothing but a long-term disaster.

When she told him she became pregnant, he threw money at her and asked her to get an abortion.

Tell a lie [Verb + Noun] *(to say something/ things that is not true)*

Susan's always telling lies.

If mark keeps telling his girlfriend lies, she will never believe him again.

The opportunity of a lifetime = a once-in-a-lifetime opportunity [Noun + Noun] *(a very good opportunity that you will only get once.)*

For many athletes, the Olympics are the opportunity of a lifetime.

A once-in-a-lifetime opportunity to travel to New York was too hard to turn down.

Take a dislike to [Verb + Noun] *(to do not like something or someone.)*

His girlfriend's father took an immediate dislike to him.

His mom took an instant dislike to his new girlfriend.

Talk sense *[Phrase] (to say something that is reasonable or sensible.)*

I couldn't talk sense to her.

Can't you talk sense?

COLLOCATIONS/U

University entry [Noun + Noun] *(an examination taken by high school graduates.)*

English is an obligatory subject for university entry.

Mary is afraid that she won't meet all requirements for university entry.

Ulterior motive [Adjective + Noun] *(a secret purpose or a hidden reason behind an action.)*

I supposed that Bob had an ulterior motive for trying to help us. He'd never helped us before.

I believe that there was no ulterior motive behind her request.

Unreliable evidence [Adjective + Noun] *(evidence that is not able to be trusted or believed.)*

It was unreliable evidence.

The defendant claimed that the letter was unreliable evidence.

Unreliable witness [Adjective + Noun] *(someone whose evidence is unlikely to be accepted or trusted in a court of law.)*

He was an unreliable witness who was caught lying a few times in Court.

I agree with you that she was an unreliable witness and not creditworthy.

Unveil a plan [Verb + Noun] *(to show or introduce a new plan to the public.)*

The police chief is ready to unveil a plan to reduce street crime at the meeting today.

The President is set to unveil a plan to fight drug abuse.

Ultimate goal [Adjective + Noun] *(a final objective or goal you want to achieve at the end of a long process.)*

Our team's ultimate goal is to be the reigning European football champion.

Richard's ultimate goal is to be the greatest dancer of all time.

Uncertain future *[Adjective + Noun] (a future that's not completely certain.)*

The people of this village probably face an uncertain future.

Many manufacturers are facing a very uncertain future in Asia.

Unique selling point *[Adjective + Noun] (a factor that is different from and better than that of the competition, such as the lowest cost, the highest quality, etc.)*

A business should look at its unique selling points compared to its competitors.

We made a list of the unique selling points that we would like to include in our advertising campaign.

Undergo surgery = undergo an operation *[Verb + Noun] (to experience or endure a medical treatment, especially an operation.)*

Jane underwent emergency surgery a few days ago after a collision with a bus.

My brother underwent major surgery on his brain last year. He will have to undergo an operation for a heart problem.

Julia underwent emergency surgery as soon as she got to the hospital.

Unemployment benefit = unemployment compensation *[Noun + Noun] (a regular payment made by the government or a labor union to help someone who can't find a job.)*

Instead of striking pay from the union, they would collect unemployment benefit.

The weekly current personal rate of unemployment benefit is approximate $157.55.

More than 3,000 people who are jobless have been filing for unemployment compensation recently.

Does she qualify for unemployment compensation?

Unfair dismissal [Adjective + Noun] *(a situation in which an employee or a worker was dismissed or fired unfairly without a good reason.)*

David is claiming unfair dismissal against his former employer on the grounds of racial discrimination.

Julie was paid $6.500 in compensation for unfair dismissal.

Unrequited love [Adjective + Noun] *(if the love that you feel for someone is unrequited, it is not shared or returned by him/her.)*

He hasn't felt very good recently mainly because of his unrequited love for a beautiful married woman.

I used to experience unrequited love when I was single.

Upset someone's stomach [Verb + Noun] *(to disturb the digestion of your stomach and make you feel sick, usually caused by something that you have eaten or drunk.)*

Jane was afraid of spicy food because it would upset her stomach.

I don't like carbonated drinks since these may upset my stomach.

Upset stomach [Adjective + Noun] *(a disorder of digestive function of your stomach which makes you sick.)*

She was suffering from an upset stomach.

He had an upset stomach after eating that spicy food.

Urban development [Adjective + Noun] *(an urban area such as a town or a city that has been developed and improved by building.)*

A lot of urban development has appeared these days.

A huge amount of urban development has been impacted by the approach of the local government recently.

Urban renewal = urban regeneration [Adjective + Noun] *(a construction program to replace or restore old buildings or buildings that are in bad condition in an urban area.)*

My aunt stayed until her house was condemned for urban renewal in 1991.

The urban renewal programme of the city has been embarked successfully.

Used car = secondhand car *[Adjective + Noun] (a car that's been previously owned by someone; not a new car.)*

The prices of used cars are always much cheaper than new ones.

I bought a secondhand car with the price of just 4,000 us dollars.

Utterly ridiculous *[Adverb + Adjective] (extremely silly or unreasonable.)*

You'll look utterly ridiculous in that short skirt.

I thought his idea was utterly ridiculous.

Upmarket shops *[Noun + Noun] (expensive fashionable shops that sell very high-quality goods and products for people who are quite rich.)*

Mason is a kind of upmarket shop.

I bought these clothes in an upmarket shop.

Unspoilt countryside *[Adjective + Noun] (countryside that has not been changed or not having a lot of modern buildings.)*

Not many people like to live and work in a place where there is unspoilt countryside.

A region with unspoilt countryside is ideal for a weekend break.

Under pressure *[Phrase] (in a state of anxiety or stress, usually because of having too much work to do.)*

We both work well under pressure.

Peter is under pressure to find a solution for his problem.

Unconditional love *[Adjective + Noun] (love without any conditions or requirements.)*

Our parents gave us unconditional love though we didn't always deserve it.

Bill says his dogs give him unconditional love, but I think they just love his food.

COLLOCATIONS/V

Voluntary work *[Adjective + Noun] (work that is done willingly, without being paid.)*

Susan does voluntary work at the local hospital two days a week.

My uncle has done voluntary work for a charity since he retired from the company.

Vehicle emissions *[Noun + Noun] (emissions produced by vehicles.)*

The government must take action to cut harmful vehicle emissions.

The government should take measures to reduce vehicle emissions immediately.

Vague idea *[Adjective + Noun] (an idea which is not clearly expressed or described.)*

He only had a vague idea of where he was, but he couldn't remember exactly.

I haven't watched this film, but I have a vague idea of what it's about.

Vague memory *[Adjective + Noun] (a memory which is unclear or incomplete.)*

He's only got a vague memory of what the hotel look liked.

Last night I was drunk, so I've only got a vague memory of what happened.

Valid point *[Adjective + Noun] (a point that most people would find logical, reasonable and generally accepted.)*

Some of his points sound valid during the discussion.

I don't think that is a valid point.

Valid reason = valid excuse *[Adjective + Noun] (a reason or excuse that most people would find reasonable, believable, and generally accepted.)*

The government put forward many valid reasons for not advertising tobacco and alcoholic drinks.

Most passenger certainly would not accept this as a valid excuse for the delay.

You must have a valid excuse for being late.

Valuable contribution [Adjective + Noun] (a very useful or helpful contribution.)

Albert Einstein made a large number of valuable contributions to the field of science.

Volunteers make many valuable contributions in this country.

Valuable information [Adjective + Noun] (very important or useful information.)

He provided the police with valuable information about the murder case.

The book provides valuable information in the fight against cancer and heart disease.

Valuable lesson [Adjective + Noun] (if an experience becomes a valuable lesson, it teaches you something important.)

The film taught me a valuable lesson.

My father taught me many valuable lessons about work and life.

Vary widely [Verb + Adverb] (to be very different.)

Prices of skin care products vary widely from shop to shop.

Education standards vary widely throughout the country.

People's taste to the spicy food can vary widely.

Vast majority [Adjective + Noun] (almost everyone or everything/ most of the people or things in a group.)

The vast majority of my father's income is passive.

The vast majority of lung cancer is related to tobacco use.

Violent crime *[Adjective + Noun] (a crime that the perpetrator uses violent force to cause injury or death to the victim.)*

There is a recent increase in violent crime in countries where guns and deadly weapons are easy to buy.

Bill was arrested for committing a violent crime.

Violent movie *[Adjective + Noun] (a movie which contains a lot of violent actions or violent scenes.)*

We don't ever allow our kids to watch violent movies.

Her husband is a big fan of violent movies.

Visiting hours *[Verb + Noun] (the period of time when you are allowed to visit someone who is in a hospital, or prison.)*

Visiting hours are between 6 and 9 p.m.

We'd better get to the hospital before visiting hours is over.

Vital organs *[Adjective + Noun] (organs in the body that are essential for life, such as the heart, lungs, brain, kidneys, and liver.)*

Vital organs will not get enough blood if blood vessels are narrowed.

Most of his vital organs are healthy, so he will live a long life.

Vital role *[Adjective + Noun] (an extremely important role.)*

The police play a vital role in ensuring (that) the law is obeyed.

Schools play a vital role in our society.

Doctors play a vital role in hospitals.

Vote against *[Verb + Adverb] (to cast a ballot against someone or something.)*

About 72 percent of the union voted against striking.

He plans to vote against Richard.

Vote for *[Phrase]* (to support someone or something with your vote)

Did you vote for or against him?

I voted for the republican candidate.

Vitamin supplement *[Noun + Noun]* (vitamins and other foods consumed in addition to nutrients in the food someone usually eats.)

She takes vitamin supplements daily.

Taking vitamin supplements is no substitute for a healthy, balanced diet.

Vegetarian food *[Noun + Noun]* (food for someone who chooses not to eat fish or meat.)

He says he prefers vegetarian food to meat and fish.

I and my mom often eat vegetarian food.

Virus infection = bacterial infection *[Noun + Noun]* (an infection caused by a virus or bacteria.)

He contracted a virus infection.

She became very ill from a bacterial infection.

Value each moment of our lives *[Phrase]* (to treasure each moment of our lives.)

We should value each moment of our lives. This is so important since we only live once.

Valuing each moment of our lives as a great gift is one of the secrets to be productive.

Volume of work *[Noun + Noun]* (the amount of work to do.)

I had a huge volume of work to do today.

He had a large volume of work on his desk to accomplish today.

COLLOCATIONS/W

Whisper softly *[Verb + Adverb] (to speak very quietly to somebody, using one's breath rather than the voice, so that other people cannot hear what you are saying.)*

She whispered softly to me that she was afraid.

Alice whispered softly to her little brother's ear.

Win an argument *[Verb + Noun] (to achieve victory in an argument)* **# lose an argument.**

Who won the argument between Jack and Jill?

He won the argument but lost the vote.

Win a scholarship *[Verb + Noun] (to gain or receive a scholarship.)*

She won a scholarship to attend Oxford University.

He won a scholarship to study law at Harvard University.

Wrongful dismissal *[Adjective + Noun] (wrongful termination of a contract of employment.)*

Tom decided to sue his employer for wrongful dismissal.

One of his employees sued him for wrongful dismissal.

Well aware of = fully aware = acutely aware *[Adverb + Verb] (fully or completely aware or informed.)*

He is well aware of the risk.

Mark is aware of the danger.

They are aware of the problem.

Wage increase *[Noun + Noun] (the amount by which a salary is increased.)*

Peter got a wage increase last month.

Joe hasn't got a wage increase so far.

Wait your turn [Verb + Noun] *(to wait until your turn to do or get something.)*

You must wait your turn like everyone else.

If you are polite, you should wait your turn.

Warm welcome [Adjective + Noun] *(a kind and friendly way you greet someone that makes them feel comfortable.)*

My co-workers gave me a very warm welcome when I returned to work.

You can always be sure of a warm welcome at our hotels.

Foreign tourists got a really warm welcome from the local people in the host country.

Warning sign [Noun + Noun] *(a sign shows that something bad or dangerous might happen.)*

What are the warning signs and symptoms of a stroke?

We should know the warning signs of fatal diseases such as a heart attack, stroke, cancer, etc.

Waste an opportunity [Verb + Noun] *(to fail to take advantage of or use of an opportunity or chance.)*

Let's not waste an opportunity to visit our parents.

I wasted many opportunities when I was in my 20s.

Waste money [Verb + Noun] *(to use money in a wrong or unnecessary way.)*

Sarah has wasted a lot of money on clothes that she hardly ever wears.

Bill wasted a large amount of money on drinking, gambling, and girls.

Waste of time [Noun + Noun] *(a bad use of time for something that's not worth spending time on.)*

Watching that film was a complete waste of time.

Asking her for money is a waste of time. She won't give you any.

Watch your weight *[Verb + Noun]* *(try not to get fat or put on weight by eating the correct foods.)*

You look overweight, so you have to be careful and watch your weight.

Lucy thinks she's a bit fat, so she's watching her weight.

Wave goodbye (to someone) *[Verb + Noun]* *(to move your hand to say goodbye to someone when they are leaving you or when you are leaving them.)*

Peter waved goodbye to me as he left.

Julie was crying when she waved goodbye to her parents.

Welcome change *[Adjective + Noun]* *(a change that you are pleased to have, receive, etc.)*

A holiday would make a welcome change from the usual routine.

It was a hot summer, so the cool weather made a welcome change.

Well after *[Adverb + Adverb]* *(much later than a particular event or period.)*

John waited outside until well after midnight.

It happened well after she graduated from high school.

Well ahead *[Adverb + Adverb]* *(further advanced than someone or something/ much earlier or sooner than someone or something.)*

Jane is trying to finish her doctoral thesis well ahead of the deadline.

Jack finished the race well ahead of the other racers.

Well aware (of) = fully aware = acutely aware *[Adverb + Adjective]* *(having full knowledge or understanding about a situation or fact.)*

I'm well aware of his strengths and weaknesses.

We are well aware of the problems of our current situation.

Well before [Adjective + Adverb] *(at a long time before the present.)*

I read this book well before he bought it.

Jessica doesn't know how old the school is, but she knows that it was built well before she was born.

Mary left the party well before her ex-boyfriend got there.

Well behind [Adjective + Adverb] *(less advanced than someone or something.)*

Tom is well behind his classmates in reading and listening skills.

I'm well behind my roommates in technology.

Well worth [Adverb + Adjective] *(be certainly deserving of something or doing something.)*

Your idea is well worth consideration.

Athol castle is well worth a visit.

Whole thing [Adjective + Noun] *(the entire thing/ all of something.)*

The kids ate the whole thing of a huge birthday cake.

We decided to cancel the plan and forget the whole thing.

Wide awake [Adverb + Adjective] *(completely or fully awake.)*

I'm always wide awake when I'm driving.

My kids were still wide awake even though it was quite late.

Wide open [Adverb + Adjective] *(fully open/ open to the full extent (of doors, windows, eyes))*

His mouth was wide open while he was sleeping.

She left the windows wide open.

Wide range = wide selection [Adjective + Noun] *(including a large number or variety of different things of the same general type; many different types of people.)*

We sell a wide range of perfumes and skin-care products.

We offer a wide range of services for the tourists.

The museum attracts a wide range of people from all walks of life.

Widely used *[Adverb + Verb] (used by a lot of people, or in a lot of places.)*

The internet and cell phones are widely used these days.

English is used more and more widely nowadays.

Widely accepted *[Adverb + Verb] (believed by many people.)*

His theories on genetics are no longer widely accepted.

Credit cards have been widely accepted these days.

Wild animal *[Adjective + Noun] (an animal that's living in a natural environment and not under human control and care.)*

Lions, tigers, and zebras are wild animals.

The government should take measures to protect wild animals that are on the verge of extinction.

Win a game *[Verb + Noun] (to beat or to defeat everyone else in a game.)*

Who do you think will win the game?

He has won 5 games so far.

Note: similar collocations include "win a contest", "win a match", "win a race", "win a tournament", "win a competition", etc.

Win an award *[Verb + Noun] (to get or receive an award.)*

Thomas won the award for best actor last year.

He cried when he won the award for best artist.

Work hard *[Verb + Adverb] (to work with a lot of effort and energy.)*

My sister always works hard at the office.

Jane doesn't mind working hard if she gets well paid.

Work well [Verb + Adverb] (to operate in a successful or satisfactory way.)

My car was quite old, but it's still working well.

This smart phone works quite well.

Worth a fortune [Verb + Noun] (worth a very large amount of money.)

These old paintings are worth a fortune.

This collection of gold jewelry must be worth a fortune.

Wrong number [Adjective + Noun] (an incorrect telephone number.)

I'm sorry, but I suppose that you've dialed the wrong number.

Did you enter the wrong number?

Warm smile [Adjective + Noun] (a friendly and loving smile.)

Jack gave Lucy a warm smile.

Carol greeted us with a warm smile.

Window seat [Noun + Noun] (a seat in a plane, bus, or train that is next to a window.)

When I got on the plane, I had a window seat.

Would you prefer a window seat or an aisle seat?

Wireless hotspot [Adjective + Noun] (a place where you can you can use a computer, mobile phone, etc. To access the internet without using wires.)

Our hotel is equipped with a wireless hotspot for guests traveling with laptops.

I usually catch up with news by using the local wireless hotspot on my smartphone.

Wireless network *[Adjective + Noun] (a network where users can use computers and other devices to access the internet without using fixed cables in order to send and receive information to each other.)*

It's very necessary to develop a high-speed wireless network system.

You must know the password if you want to access the wireless network on the school campus.

Wine and dine *[Phrase] (to entertain someone by providing them with expensive food and drink.)*

We were wined and dined at a fancy restaurant and given the best hotel last night.

She's planning to wine and dine me, but she won't be inviting him.

Working conditions *[Adjective + Noun] (the conditions which are connected with your job, such as cleanliness, lighting, equipment, safety, levels of noise, stress, paid overtime, uniforms, access to amenities, etc.)*

Working conditions in the factory have significantly improved since workers threatened to go on strike.

The workers asked for better working conditions but their demands were not accepted.

Weather forecast *[Noun + Noun] (a statement usually broadcast on television, radio or in a newspaper saying what the weather will be like for a period of time in the future.)*

According to the weather forecast, it will rain next week.

Have you heard tomorrow's weather forecast?

Window shopping *[Noun + Noun] (the activity of looking at the goods displayed in the windows of shops without making any purchases.)*

We went window shopping last night.

Window shopping is her favorite pastime.

Word of mouth *[Phrase] (recommendations that people verbally make to each other about a product of service.)*

Word of mouth has made this film a hit.

The novel has become a worldwide best-seller, largely by word of mouth.

Most customers hear about his company by word of mouth.

Worth reading book *[Adjective + Noun] (a book that is beneficial to read.)*

My daughter loves this book from the day she has it. It is a definitely worth reading book.

There is no doubt that it is a worth reading book, so just read it.

Widespread flooding *[Adjective + Noun] (large amounts of water covering many places.)*

There are reports of widespread flooding in Qatar.

Widespread flooding is affecting many countries in southern Africa.

Well-built body *[Adjective + Noun] (a body that is strong and attractive.)*

He hits the gym every day, so he has a fairly well-built body.

Her husband has short black hair and a well-built body.

Watery eyes *[Adjective + Noun] (eyes containing or filled with tears.)*

Jessica dabbed her watery eyes with a piece of tissue.

She was looking at him with watery eyes.

Worried sick *[Phrase] (extremely worried.)*

His parents were worried sick about him.

She and her husband are worried sick about her daughter.

Whisper softly *[Verb + Noun] (to say something very quietly so that other people cannot hear what you are saying.)*

"I had a great time tonight, Mary," he whispered softly

'When can I see you again?' she whispered softly.

Weigh up options *[Verb + Noun] (to consider the good and bad aspects of each option.)*

He always weighs up options along with the benefits and risks before making an important decision.

It's very important to stop and think, or to weigh up options before making a decision.

COLLOCATIONS/XYZ

X-ray vision [Noun + Noun] *(the ability to see inside or through objects that are not transparent.)*

I don't believe he has x-ray vision.

Doctors don't have x-ray vision, but they have x-ray machines.

Yawning gap [Verb + Noun] *(a gap which is very wide or extremely large and difficult to reduce.)*

A yawning gap between the rich and the poor still exists nowadays in many countries.

There's still a yawning gap between workers' pay and productivity.

Yet again [Adverb + Adverb] *(one more time, after many other times.)*

The flight was delayed yet again.

Prices of gas increased yet again.

Youthful enthusiasm [Adjective + Noun] *(a great enthusiasm that is typical of young people.)*

I really admired your youthful enthusiasm for sciences.

Peter has managed to maintain his youthful enthusiasm for literature.

Youth hostel [Noun + Noun] *(a place providing cheap accommodation for short periods to young people when they are travelling.)*

Could you please show me where the youth hostel is?

We shared a room in the youth hostel.

Youthful appearance [Adjective + Noun] *(to look young.)*

He has a youthful appearance.

She tried to maintain her youthful appearance by using sunblock every day.

Zero tolerance *[Adjective + Noun]* *(the policy of applying laws or penalties to every person who commits a crime or breaks a rule, even minor infringements of a code.)*

The police announced that there will be zero tolerance for abuse and violence against women.

Tom was caught stealing a woman's bag, and because of zero tolerance, he was sent to prison for 3 years.

Zero visibility *[Adjective + Noun]* *(the condition when someone is literally unable to see anything due to darkness, poor weather, fog and/or smoke.)*

Driving in zero visibility is risky.

I'm sure that no one can walk safely in zero visibility.

Conclusion

Thank you again for downloading this book on *"Shortcut To English Collocations: Master 2000+ English Collocations In Used Explained Under 20 Minutes A Day."* and reading all the way to the end. I'm extremely grateful.

If you know of anyone else who may benefit from the informative tips presented in this book, please help me inform them of this book. I would greatly appreciate it.

Finally, if you enjoyed this book and feel that it has added value to your life in any way, please take a couple of minutes to share your thoughts and post a REVIEW on Amazon. Your feedback will help me to continue to write the kind of Kindle books that helps you get results. Furthermore, if you write a simple REVIEW with positive words for this book on Amazon, you can help hundreds or perhaps thousands of other readers who may want to improve their English skills sounding like a native speaker. Like you, they worked hard for every penny they spend on books. With the information and recommendation you provide, they would be more likely to take action right away. We really look forward to reading your review.

Thanks again for your support and good luck!

If you enjoy my book, please write a POSITIVE REVIEW on amazon.

-- Rachel Mitchell --

Check Out Other Books

Go here to check out other related books that might interest you:

Marriage Heat: 7 Secrets Every Married Couple Should Know On How To Fix Intimacy Problems, Spice Up Marriage & Be Happy Forever

https://www.amazon.com/dp/B01ITSW8YU

Smart Kids Smart Money: The Ultimate Parent's Guide To Teaching Kids About Earning, Saving, Giving, Spending And Investing Money Wisely

https://www.amazon.com/dp/B01N2PCQIM

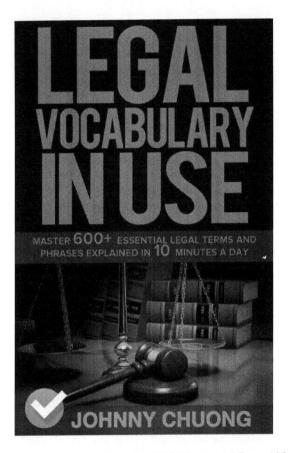

Legal Vocabulary In Use: Master 600+ Essential Legal Terms And Phrases Explained In 10 Minutes A Day

http://www.amazon.com/dp/B01L0FKXPU

English Collocations In Use: Master 500+ Collocations Explained In 10 Minutes A Day

http://www.amazon.com/dp/B01JHUNYZQ

Shortcut To Ielts Writing: The Ultimate Guide To Immediately Increase Your Ielts Writing Scores

http://www.amazon.com/dp/B01JV7EQGG

The Shocking Truth About Sexual Blackmail: The Secrets Cyber Scammers Don't Want You To Know - The World's Best Advice On How To Deal With Sexual Blackmailers

http://www.amazon.com/dp/B01IO1615Y

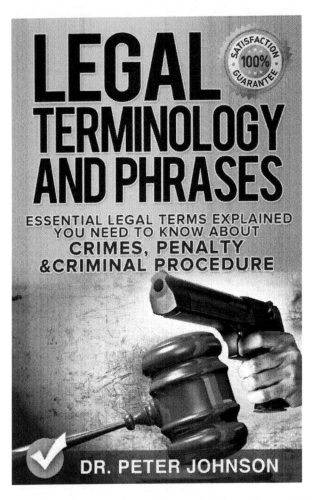

Legal Terminology And Phrases: Essential Legal Terms Explained You Need To Know About Crimes, Penalty And Criminal Procedure

http://www.amazon.com/dp/B01L5EB54Y

Legal Terminology And Phrases: Essential Legal Terms Explained You Need To Know About Civil Law And Civil Procedure

https://www.amazon.com/dp/B01LDLRU0C

Productivity Secrets For Students: The Ultimate Guide To Improve Your Mental Concentration, Kill Procrastination, Boost Memory And Maximize Productivity In Study

http://www.amazon.com/dp/B01JS52UT6

Daughter of Strife: 7 Techniques On How To Win Back Your Stubborn Teenage Daughter

https://www.amazon.com/dp/B01HS5E3V6

Parenting Teens With Love And Logic: A Survival Guide To Overcoming The Barriers Of Adolescence About Dating, Sex And Substance Abuse

https://www.amazon.com/dp/B01JQUTNPM